OPTIMISM
AT ALL
COSTS

OPTIMISM AT ALL COSTS

Black Attitudes, Activism,
and Advancement in
Obama's America

Lessie B. Branch

University of Massachusetts Press
Amherst and Boston

ISBN 978-1-62534-327-7 (paper); 326-0 (hardcover)

Designed by Sally Nichols
Set in Adobe Garamond Pro and Lato
Printed and bound by Maple Press, Inc.

Cover design by Patricia Duque Campos

Library of Congress Cataloging-in-Publication Data
A catalog record for this book is available from the Library of Congress.

British Library Cataloguing-in-Publication Data
A catalog record for this book is available from the British Library.

Portions of the introduction and of chapters 1–4 were previously published as
"Reexamining the 'Obama Effect': How Barack Obama's Rhetoric Spread
Optimistic Colorblindness in an Age of Inequality" in the *Journal of
Contemporary Rhetoric* 6, no. 3/4 (2016).
Courtesy of the Alabama Communication Association.

CONTENTS

PREFACE

In 1994, I was working as a legal administrative assistant at Goodkind Labaton Rudoff & Sucharow LLP (now Labaton Sucharow LLP), who had successfully represented Black plaintiffs in a pro bono racial discrimination case. It was disappointing to learn that in 1994, thirty years after the Civil Rights Act of 1964, the plaintiffs encountered things like nooses, swastikas, and "Whites only" signs at their work place. As a child of the 1960s, I wanted to become a civil rights attorney and join the fight against discrimination. While I was happy the plaintiffs in the case won, I wanted to see a broader response to issues of discrimination, where the framework of a more just and inclusive society could be fostered. It was at this point that I opted to attend policy school where I focused on Black racial attitudes, wrestling with the question of whether Blacks contribute to the perpetuation of discrimination they experience through internalized negative racial attitudes.

Since that time, I have determined that it is harmful to have a narrative or discourse of equality that makes race invisible but does not erase or breakdown hierarchies that perpetuate a racialized hierarchical status quo. The "Doll Test," which identified the harm of obstinate social structures that perpetuate inequality, was quickly followed by the Supreme Court decision that ended segregation, in theory. Overemphasis on individual effort and bootstrap philosophy ignores the hierarchical context of identities such as race, age, ethnicity, and their influence in both positive and negative ways. We need policies that recognize, call out, and address these hierarchies. Responding by *pathologizing* those who are socioeconomically marginalized rather than acknowledging that there is a systemic problem is shortsighted and dangerous for everyone.

Society must enact a framework of bold policies that go beyond marginal solutions and individual responses to hierarchical structures of disparity. And Blacks must hold those structures accountable through social movements that realign Black socioeconomic beliefs with their socioeconomic reality.

AUTHOR'S NOTE

I use the term *Black* to refer to African Americans and those who have "roots" in the African diaspora; they may or may not be of Hispanic or Latinx heritage. I have chosen to use *Black* as opposed to African American because the Pew Charitable Trust report that began my inquiry into the claim of ebullience also used the term *Black* to describe those reporting increased optimism. I have chosen also to capitalize the term *Black* as I use it to refer to a group of people, much the same way *Hispanic* or *Latinx* are used to refer to a group of people.

Similarly, I use the term *White* to refer to those of European descent in the same way it is used by the Pew Charitable Trust report that investigates Black optimism. Again, I capitalize this term for the same reason that I capitalize the term *Black*.

I use the terms *individualist* and *collectivist* to refer to the belief that Blacks' own hard work and responsibility result in their socioeconomic gains and the belief that Black gains are the result of a group or collective effort respectively.

ACKNOWLEDGMENTS

We spend our formative years learning to be independent and to do things on our own, yet the apostle Paul reminds us in Romans 14:7 that none of us live to ourselves or die to ourselves. The endeavor of this book reminds me of the importance of working together to achieve goals. This project is evidence of the success that happens when we engage in collective action.

My deepest thanks to Darrick Hamilton for his vision, patience, and belief in my work and for his unfailing encouragement. When it is my turn to sit in the advisor's chair, may I execute my responsibilities with clarity of vision, patience, and encouragement, as he did on my behalf. My thanks also to Lisa Servon who sparked my interest in social policy in several courses that I took with her, which ultimately led me to The New School's PhD program in public policy. My thanks also to Terry Williams, whose Visual Sociology course encouraged us to bring sociological issues to life. Your guidance in the making of my minidocumentary, *Invisibility Now Seen*, created a foundation for this current work. My thanks to Robin Hayes for the important scholarship regarding social movements and your help in informing this important area of my own scholarship. To the external reviewers of my manuscript, I am grateful for your insight and words of encouragement about the importance, need, and timeliness of this work and for your wisdom in helping it to become more polished. To Brian Halley and the faculty board at the University of Massachusetts Press, I am thankful for your approval to publish this work. Thanks also to Ellen Daldoss for her eagle eyes in proofreading and editing.

To my husband, David Lamont Branch, I thank you so much for being my best friend and a constant source of encouragement as I juggled the responsibilities of life and working to see this project to fruition. Thanks also for creating a conceptual image for the book cover. I am truly grateful for having you in my life.

To my son, David Lamont Branch II, I've accomplished and achieved many things, but you are by far the accomplishment of which I am proudest. You, my handsome Prince, are the apple of my eye. I love you very much. In some ways, my endeavor in this work, in the words of Regina Belle's "If I Could" (our theme song) is "to try to change the world I brought you to."

To my parents, Bishop Mamie L. Raji and Pastor Busari A. Raji Sr., thank you both for being my parents. Your examples have taught me that faith without works is not fruitful. I have tried to carry on your legacy by living the life lessons you have taught me. I hope I have made you proud.

To my sister, Grace L. Patterson, in a world of chaos, you were the one to follow! Because you kept your bearing true, I had an example to follow. You are my Harriet Tubman; you rescued me.

OPTIMISM
AT ALL
COSTS

The Paradoxical Ebullience Problem

I remember being euphoric over the 2008 election of Barack Obama as America's forty-fourth president. I stayed up late and watched the projections and returns declaring him the winner. I was hopeful for America as a country, that the economy would get better, and that President Obama would keep the promise he made as a senator when he addressed the NAACP to fight for Black folk as so many fought for him. I was also hopeful that maybe America was turning the corner and embracing the pledge made by the framers of the Declaration of Independence that "all men are created equal."

On my journey to earn a doctorate in public policy with the goal of working toward a fairer and inclusive society, I believed these ideals of equality could be observed in American society, but I had doubts. The election of Barack Obama called those doubts into question. About a year into Obama's presidency, reports about the unbridled optimism among Blacks on their improved quality of life and future prospects were circulating widely. I didn't share that optimism and several colleagues and friends told me they found it odd that I was "anti-Obama." I explained that I was not "anti-Obama," but conflating his election with Black well-being puts Blacks in a precarious position regarding their well-being, diverts attention away from the challenges facing Blacks, gives Obama a pass on keeping his promise to Black America, to fight for them, and lets those who have negatively impacted that well-being off the hook. Simply put, Obama's election to the presidency did not erase the centuries of accumulated disparity to which Blacks have been shackled, and it certainly didn't erase the losses of the Great Recession.

Since roughly the mid-1990s, Blacks have become steadily more optimistic about their socioeconomic prospects, with a sharp spike in optimism beginning in 2007. However, data indicate that Black socioeconomic status has not improved relative to that of Whites. There is a demonstrable concern that this *paradoxical ebullience*—the gap between Black relative socioeconomic position and their racial attitudes—may stymie Black socioeconomic progress in the United States. Specifically, Black optimism that belies Black socioeconomic reality may disempower the collective action social change requires.

A report by the Pew Charitable Trust in 2010 found that Blacks' assessment of their own economic progress in America had improved more dramatically between 2007 and 2009 than at any other time during the previous twenty-five years. The report noted that Black ebullience coincided neatly with the election of Barack Obama, "despite a deep recession and jobless recovery that have hit blacks especially hard." Indeed, the study found that 39 percent of Blacks in 2009 believed they were "better off than they were in the previous five years," whereas only 20 percent of Blacks believed this in 2007. It also reported that a majority of Blacks (56 percent) said that the standard-of-living gap between Whites and Blacks narrowed in the past decade.[1]

The economic data tell a different story. Two key indicators of Black socioeconomic well-being are unemployment and wealth. In these two areas, Blacks fare poorly relative to Whites. Since 1972, when the Bureau of Labor Statistics began collecting information on labor force characteristics by demographics, including race and ethnicity, the population of unemployed Blacks has been twice that of unemployed Whites.[2] Yet despite this gap in Black-White unemployment Blacks have become more optimistic about their relative socioeconomic standing. Since 1972 there has been only one time (2000) when Black unemployment fell below 8 percent. Conversely, there have been fewer than five times when the White unemployment rate climbed above 8 percent.[3]

In terms of wealth, since the annual Survey of Income and Program Participation (SIPP) began in 1984, Whites have never had less than seven times the wealth of Blacks. (The low occurred in 1995.) Since 1984, the ratio remained for two decades between ten to one and twelve to one, Whites to Blacks. But the last time the gap was in that range was in 2004. In 2009, the White to Black wealth gap hit a high of nineteen to one. Again, in spite of this data, a majority of Blacks in the Pew study said that the standard-of-living gap between Whites and Blacks narrowed in the past decade. As of 2011, for every dollar of wealth Whites had, Blacks only had six cents.[4] These data highlight a paradoxical discordance between Black racial attitudes and their actual economic progress. Paradoxical ebullience may be responsible for limited Black collective action observed in the twenty-first century to address stagnating Black economic parity, and it may contribute to a reversal of gains made since 1964.

One possible explanation of this paradox is the well-known phenomenon of partisan bias in evaluations of the economy. There is a robust body of evidence showing that Americans, regardless of race, tend to view the economy in a more positive light when the president's political affiliation matches their own; in other words, Democrats exhibit a more positive assessments of the economy when there is a Democrat in the White House, and vice versa for Republicans.[5] Because 80 percent of American Blacks lean Democrat (with 64 percent identifying as registered Democrats),[6] we might expect Black opinions about the economy to become more favorable when a Democrat is president, such as Obama (who was in office at the time the Pew poll was conducted).

Although this phenomenon may provide a partial explanation

of paradoxical ebullience, it is not clear that it is enough by itself to account for Blacks' optimism. The most striking evidence that something else is afoot is that the rise in optimism coinciding with Obama's election was more dramatic than any rise in optimism among Blacks since 1984. Even when Democrat Bill Clinton was elected in 1992 and again in 1996, Blacks' opinion of their socioeconomic standing remained more moderate. Therefore, the partisan-bias hypothesis cannot fully explain paradoxical ebullience. Rather, we must look to more complex social, political, and discursive trends to find the roots of this strange phenomenon. Such complex trends are the subject of the analysis in this book.

What, if not simple partisan bias, is responsible for contemporary Blacks' ebullient attitudes? Does paradoxical ebullience result from a shift in Black racial attitudes away from the pursuit of common socioeconomic goals and toward a more individualist, less collectivist posture based on post-racial discourse?[7] If so, why has this shift occurred? Can such a shift have political ramifications that hurt Blacks economically? To help answer these questions, I explore how contemporary, post-racial Black narratives compare with civil rights and Black Power narratives.

In this book, I argue that Black ebullience and individualistic attitudes diminish Black collective action and perpetuate socioeconomic stagnation, and that a dwindling of collectivist attitudes among Blacks jeopardizes policies that provide socioeconomic benefits to Blacks. My goal is to argue that ebullience is reinforced by a complex interaction between elite racial narratives and the everyday psychology of race, which together are powerful enough to overcome a simple awareness of the facts. As we shall see in due course, new developments like the Black Lives Matter movement may be opening up new possibilities for non-elite discourse. For the time being, however, it appears that Blacks' optimism is born out of a combination of an identification with optimistic Black elites and a desire to survive and thrive in the face of everyday racism.

This book focuses on the eight years of Obama's presidency, which are especially relevant to considerations of elite Black discourse and shifts in optimism. The relationship between paradoxical ebullience and the Obama presidency was complex, and we must understand how shifts in public opinion both are and are not attributable to the historic election of America's first Black president. However, before we can clearly understand the narratives that contribute to Black ebullience and how these have shifted in recent decades, we need to understand the philosophical and critical background of race.

A BRIEF HISTORY OF RACIAL DISCOURSE

Only within the broader context of race theory and its development will we be able to clearly assess the implications, innuendos, and social impacts of contemporary race narratives. This is not intended to be a comprehensive account of the development of contemporary racial ideologies and understandings. Rather my goal is to introduce readers to what are relatively recent notions of race, in order to demonstrate that many theories of racial inequality are rooted in political and philosophical ideology instead of social realities. With this understanding in place, we can better see the political and philosophical motivations behind our contemporary theories of inequality, which are discussed in chapter 1.

The Early Beginnings of Racial Discourse

The term *race* did not take on its modern meaning until the seventeenth century. At that time Europeans were exploring the planet and encountering others with markedly different physical appearances. In 1684, François Bernier, a physician who traveled the world, described what is commonly, though not universally, believed to be the first expression of the modern concept of race: "There are four or five species or races of men in particular whose difference is so remarkable that it may be properly made use of as the foundation of a new division of the earth."[8] Bernier suggested these races existed due to hereditary differences, but this understanding of race was not the politically and morally charged notion that it quickly became.

The addition of political and moral elements to the concept of race is traceable to the philosophical/religious idea of a hierarchy of creation. According to this idea, there is a necessary difference between the races because God created the world according to a specific order. This view that racial difference is somehow inevitable in nature continues to have reverberations in racial discourse today. The Swedish naturalist Carolus Linnaeus (1707–1778) expressed this idea clearly in his system of classification of the natural world, in which he attempted to explain that God created the world according to an order where White Europeans were closest to perfection. Linnaeus's description of the African race parallels contemporary stereotypes of Black Americans: relaxed, indolent, negligent, and capricious—in short, lazy and irresponsible. The idea of lazy Blacks dates back even before the creation of the United States. As we progress with our analysis, we will come to understand the civil rights and Black Power era of the 1950s–1970s as a reaction against this opinion of the Black race.

Another trend that we will encounter later is the idea that Blacks should not view themselves as part of a group—that Black racial and cultural identity is, in effect, an illusion that might have detrimental consequences at the individual level. This idea has roots in eighteenth-century religious-oriented European thought as well. For example, Count Georges-Louis Buffon (1707–1788) subscribed to a theory of monogenesis, which is that all human beings descend from one original pair (consistent with the Christian story of Adam and Eve). Buffon saw climate as the most salient for causing racial differences.[9] Later, the philosopher Immanuel Kant (1724–1804) supported the view that racial difference was merely a matter of circumstance and that all humans, regardless of race, should be striving toward the same goals (for Kant, the goal of "civilization").[10] Kant also described a need for those of African descent to rely on those of European descent to help them attain those goals—an idea we will recognize in much of the post-racial discourse today.

This view of race justifies a color-blind belief that individual Blacks should not view themselves as part of a group and should not embrace group identity. Thus, both the idea that Blacks are somehow culturally inferior and the idea that Blacks have nothing but circumstance to bind them together as a group are effectively European ideas that have made their way, albeit in modified form, into present-day discourse. We see in the early development of racial discourse a placement of Blacks in an inferior position, followed by a move that effectively strips Blacks of their collective racial identity by minimizing racial divisions and claiming that they are not static or real. As I will argue in later chapters, Black elites who argue against Black collective identity are effectively echoing the racist views of these European thinkers.

Racism in Early American Elite Discourse

Turning to the United States, we begin to see how influential elite discourse can be in establishing ideas about racial difference and (in)equality. The United States' third president, Thomas Jefferson (1743–1826), was one of the first writers to explicitly compare Blacks unfavorably to Whites. He suspected that Blacks, "are inferior to the white in the endowments both of body and mind."[11] In his *Notes on the State of Virginia* (1787), Jefferson made value claims regarding the cultural contributions of Blacks. Such claims, propounded by Jefferson and other early American elites, were made permanent fixtures of American thought when they were disseminated as established knowledge. For example, the *Encyclopedia Britannica* (1798) described the "negro race" as ugly, misshapen, prone to vice, unhappy, idle, and so on.

Traditionally, people trusted encyclopedias to provide objective, neutral, unbiased accounts. Many viewed them as definitive sources of truth. Imagine a White person in 1800 who had no direct experience of Blacks looking at this definition in order to understand the truth of the "negro race." Elite discourse descended to common knowledge when the public read that Blackness was a mark of being uncivilized and criminal. In the twenty-first century, we can clearly perceive the racist value system operative in this encyclopedia entry. But at the time it was published this definition would likely have been taken for objective fact, hence influencing the opinions and actions of the mass of educated Americans. Over time, those educated Americans influenced policy and social structures, and thus these perceptions of race became entrenched, leading to the vast inequalities we still observe today.

The Inevitability of Inequality

The deeply entrenched view of Blacks as lazy and irresponsible can, as I will argue in later chapters, be a self-fulfilling prophecy when it is paired with the idea that inequality is inevitable. Although there are contemporary arguments for the inevitability of inequality that focus on personal traits and the economic structure of capitalism, these modern arguments may be mere justifications of an older, more ideological belief about inequality. There are many different arguments for inevitability of inequality, and it would be neither practical nor productive to attempt to describe them all here. Instead, I will focus on just one that continues to reverberate in today's academic and political discourse: the dialectical view of inequality articulated by the German philosopher Georg Wilhelm Friedrich Hegel (1770–1831). Hegel argued that because different races have different geographical origins and because different geographical regions have been important at different times in history, history is necessarily racialized.[12] Hegel's view implied that, if the

White race has historically had more power than the Black race, this power differential is not only acceptable, but a necessary component of the unfolding of history.

Hegel was describing, fundamentally, the idea that history has a purpose and that, through its ups and downs, humanity is always improving overall.[13] As we shall see later, the belief that conditions are improving and that there are no struggles left is one of the key ideas used to justify a position of blaming Black Americans for their socioeconomic difficulties. It is clear from Hegel's discourse that this idea is not a new one. We must also note that Hegel, like many of his predecessors, provided a philosophical basis for justifying, or naturalizing, inequality. Hegel's justification, rather than relying on biological differences among the races, relied on historical progress. In my analysis of the works of Martin Luther King Jr. and others, we will see this type of naturalization can be directly responsible for diminishing the extent to which individuals and collectives feel motivated and empowered to act on their own behalf.

American Race Theory is Born

By the 1850s, theories of race were abundant, particularly in the scientific fields. Several authors, such as Arthur de Gobineau and Robert Knox, suggested that racial characteristics—including cultural characteristics—were innate, and that Blacks were the lowest among the races. In 1859, Charles Darwin (1809–1882) published the groundbreaking *Origin of Species by Means of Natural Selection, or The Preservation of Favoured Races in the Struggle for Life,* which reinforced the idea that Blacks could and should strive toward the same degree of "civilization" as Whites. Francis Galton (1822–1911), who is considered "the father of eugenics," argued that the Black race was incapable of producing a genius.

At the same time, other writers continued to attempt to erase the notion of racial classification. In 1911, Franz Boas published

The Mind of Primitive Man, a text in which he tried to undermine the scientific reliability of the concept of race using IQ tests.[14] By the 1940s and 1950s, several scholars—such as Ruth Benedict, who was influenced by Boas and cowrote *The Races of Mankind* (1948)—had worked hard to undermine the belief in pure races and to make anthropologists and other social scientists aware of the deficient evidence for classifying races.

In the early twentieth century, both racist ideas of racial difference (descended from Linnaeus and others) and racist ideas of racial nonexistence (descended from Buffon) were at a pinnacle, perhaps finally creating space for voices to speak out against the centuries-long history of scholarly denigration of the Black race. In *The Souls of Black Folk* (1903), W. E. B. Du Bois (1868–1963) stated that "the problem of the Twentieth Century is the problem of the color-line,—the relation of the darker to the lighter races of men in Asia and Africa, in America and the islands of the sea."[15] Although Du Bois was one of the first to attempt to contradict some of the racist thinking of earlier centuries, he also believed that Africans and descendants of Africans would become the next historically significant people, a view that can be seen as a modification of Hegel. Du Bois also suggested that cultural beliefs and practices were more significant than race. Although this represented a shift away from the biological view of race, it may be seen as a precursor to color-blind racism. Still, throughout the twentieth century, shifting the focus to culture, in part as a result of the discourse of Du Bois and others, opened up new ways of thinking about race.[16]

Thinking of race as a cultural descriptor potentially bypasses the racism found in earlier classification systems, even those based on nonegalitarian cultural differences. This helped open up space to consider the ways in which race is socially constructed, how that construction gets mapped onto bodies, and how persons receive advantage and disadvantage while, at the same time, refusing to reduce racial difference to mere biological difference. Such a cultural focus paved the way for the civil rights and Black Power eras, as well as for the theoretical framework of critical race theory, as we shall see. Whether these ideological gains have been fully accepted by the American populace is a crucial question we shall examine in detail in future chapters.

Before considering the recent discussions about the possibility of a post-racial society, we ought to consider the notion of *racial formation* put forth by Michael Omi and Howard Winant in their 1986 book *Racial Formation in the United States*. This idea begins to dissolve the tension we have traced in this introduction between a biological view of race and a view of race as illusory. They defined race as "a concept which signifies and symbolizes social conflicts and interests by referring to different types of human bodies."[17] The focus is on the social significance attributed to the body, rather than the body itself. Which phenotypes are the most salient for determining one's race are established through sociohistorical processes. Instead of understanding race as an innate, concrete essence on the one hand, or as illusory on the other, Omi and Winant tried to show that race is contingently given social significance, often in an arbitrarily hierarchical way. Racial formation is "the sociohistorical process by which racial categories are created, inhabited, transformed, and destroyed."[18] Put differently, we may want to focus on racialized groups, that is, groups to whom racial significance has been given (whether positive or negative), instead of races, which may not actually exist.

If racialization is a process that occurs within a sociohistorical context, then racism becomes something we can manage. In other words, race and racism are not universal, transhistorical features of our species. Therefore, we can assume that, because things were different in the past, they can be different in the future. Of course, there are hurdles. First, the popular mind still thinks of race quite differently from the scholarly discourse on race. For example, claiming that race has no biological basis is still met with much skepticism among the masses. Second, there are a host of institutions that perpetuate the racial hierarchy of White normativity and White privilege. These ideas may permeate, by way of public discourse, into the Black consciousness, as well, preventing or discouraging Blacks from engaging in the collective action that may be necessary to enact change.

CHAPTER 1

Post-Racial Theories of Racial Inequality

The ideologies through which Black elites interpret racism change according to the demands of social and political contexts. During the pre–civil rights, civil rights and Black power eras, Black elite discourse emphasized collective action and common fate. But in today's "post-racial" society, discourse on racial inequality emphasizes color blindness and laissez-faire racism, and post-racialism literature demonstrates a trend among Blacks (including elites) to interpret socioeconomic progress (or lack thereof) less in terms of collective action and more in terms of individual initiative. These concepts developed through the social sciences, and theories of color blindness and color-blind racism came to influence Black attitudes. What is the meaning and importance of these emerging race concepts for the Black common fate and collective action? How do they relate to Black socioeconomic parity? How have theorists effected a shift away from former ideas of race and generated buy-in for the post-racial view of society?

CONTEMPORARY CONCEPTS OF RACE: COLOR BLINDNESS, LAISSEZ-FAIRE RACISM, AND POST-RACIALISM

Scholars today conduct a more nuanced discussion of race, but many still subscribe to a clichéd notion of progress that assumes that the dominant White culture is a standard to which all groups should strive to attain. As we shall see later in this chapter and in the following chapter, assuming that Blacks want to conform to the dominant culture is highly problematic. Contemporary concepts of race have, over the past decades, exhibited a tendency toward erasing racial difference, assuming as a desirable goal the homogenization of culture. The mechanisms by which commentators propose to accomplish such homogenization vary; some propose that individual "color-blind" perceptions are required to erase difference, whereas others see the "solution" as an economic one. In all cases, the fundamental, unspoken assumption is that Blacks and Whites should become not only socioeconomically equal but functionally indistinguishable. This attitude takes as its point of departure the White culture and way of life, implicitly forcing all other cultures into conformity and measuring their success or progress in terms of that conformity. Below, we examine in detail several contemporary theories of race. The highly questionable notion of racist progress runs as a common thread through each of them.

Color Blindness

According to psychology professor Sheri Atwater, color blindness is the notion that race should no longer matter in everyday American life. Atwater traced the notion of color blindness to the 1896 minority opinion by Justice Harlan in *Plessy v. Ferguson*, which called for equal treatment of all persons under the law.[1] Atwater asserted that the Thirteenth and Fourteenth Amendments to the U.S. Constitution enabled color blindness. The Thirteenth Amendment outlawed slavery, and the Fourteenth Amendment decreed that all persons born in the United States are citizens of the United States and of their state of residence. It also holds that no state can deny citizens of the United States equal protection under the law. In theory, these amendments granted Blacks the same rights enjoyed by Whites. In 1896, Plessy argued that Louisiana was in violation of the

Constitution because it required Blacks to ride in train cars that were separate from the train cars reserved for White passengers. Although Justice Harlan's minority opinion was culturally influential, the court decided in a majority of seven to one that the "separate but equal" law did not violate the Thirteenth and Fourteenth Amendments by permitting the unequal treatment of Blacks.

The premise of color blindness is that justice, and all laws, should ignore skin color. But Atwater argued that this notion has been transmogrified, in everyday parlance, into the idea that race does not matter. Therefore, de jure nondiscrimination has devolved into de facto denial of racial issues altogether. Along these lines, Eduardo Bonilla-Silva argued that color-blind discourse is in fact detrimental to racial harmony in that it disallows the consideration or even discussion of race.[2] It also allows stakeholders to hold racist or biased perceptions tacitly while they espouse a color-blind ethos of race relations through frames that offer alternative, false reasons for Black inequality.

Color blindness normalizes the racial disparity in accumulated socioeconomic disadvantages experienced by Blacks as a Black problem, the failure of Blacks to work hard and be responsible for their success, rather than framing the disparity as an indication of structural racism. Acceptance of the concept of color blindness influences Blacks to orient their attitudes away from collective action as the means to address the group's outcomes and toward an individualistic posture that rationalizes the disparate outcomes experienced by Blacks as the result of their own lack of effort and responsibility. The fact that Black socioeconomic disparity is caused by systemic problems deadens the effect of individual Black efforts; therefore, Blacks' purely economic, individual efforts to ameliorate their socioeconomic status are largely fruitless. Though it seems unlikely, many Black people have themselves adopted the attitude of color blindness, thereby mimicking the values and attitudes of Whites in an assimilationist manner.

Laissez-Faire Racism

The adoption of color blindness among Blacks may enable a less overt, but more pervasive, form of racism known as laissez-faire racism. Laissez-faire racism is the view that Blacks are the cause of their own economic stagnation because they refuse to engage in the equal opportunities that they have been afforded and are therefore undeserving of special government support.[3] Unlike state-sanctioned racism, laissez-faire racism is based on the market and on informal racial bias. That is to say, rather than an active, "hands-on" approach to Black racism (think Jim Crow), laissez-faire racism is a "hands-off" approach that operates to discriminate against those who are market outsiders owing to differences in parameters like hard work, frugality, and personal responsibility, which White society uses to explain economic success. Similarly, sociologists Eric Tranby and Douglas Hartmann have argued that by framing racial disparities in terms of individualism, free will, relationalism, and anti-structuralism, laissez-faire racism advances the belief that inequality is based on problems in Blacks themselves, and not in racist U.S. institutions or society.[4] The ideology of laissez-faire racism informs the American racial narrative about Black socioeconomic parity and future progress. Laissez-faire racism dismisses the possibility of structures or institutions dedicated to the marginalization of Blacks.

Post-Racialism

Much discussion about America's entrance into a post-racial era centered on the 2008 election of Barack Obama. There seemed to be a popular belief that the success of such personalities as Oprah Winfrey and the election of Obama indicated that race no longer mattered in America. But other scholars have debated the truth of this notion. Law professor Michèle Alexandre (not to be confused with civil rights author Michelle Alexander), for example, has highlighted several areas of American life where

Blacks continue to suffer disproportionate disadvantages.[5] These areas of disparity between Whites and Blacks include a lack of access to job opportunities and to educational equality. Additionally, Blacks comprise a disproportionate segment of the prison population relative to their numbers in the general population. Furthermore, in the recent economic crisis, Blacks have experienced higher rates of foreclosures and unemployment. The underlying purpose of post-racial discourse may be to ignore these disparities.

One of the tenets of post-racialism is that one's identity is no longer bounded by race, but can expand beyond that framework. But according to Alexandre most government forms still collect demographic information, including those that determine eligibility for social assistance programs and educational aid, which require respondents to identify their race. This trend may also influence electoral advantages at the district level.[6] Thus, while on an abstract level it may be argued that identity has moved beyond race, race is still the basis on which funding is allocated. Alexandre wisely asserted that the formal bureaucratic recognition of Blacks as a distinct, disadvantaged group should remind Blacks of their common ground as a social group.

Post-Blackness

This discussion of contemporary views of race would be incomplete without an acknowledgment of the emerging "post-black" theory. Post-Blackness emerged from the work of Touré, who argued that Blackness in contemporary America is a highly individualized and multifaceted characteristic.[7] According to Touré, there are many different ways to be Black, and focusing on Blackness as a single, collective identity threatens to delegitimize individual expressions of Blackness, especially when those expressions run counter to dominant ideas of what collective Blackness "should" look like. By emphasizing that Blackness can take an infinite number of forms, the theory of post-Blackness attempts to liberate individual Blacks without overlooking the importance of race as a component of individual identity. Thereby, this theory might be viewed as overcoming the limitations of post-racialism by acknowledging the existence of Blackness as a social and economic category but unlinking it from performative identity requirements.

Critics of Touré and of post-Blackness have argued that Blacks, no matter how individual their identity, are linked historically by their common ancestry and the history of race in the United States. As Stephanie Li puts it, "Awareness of history and its relationship to black identity is notably lacking in Touré's totalizing claims. With its emphasis on individualist expressions of racial identity, post-blackness threatens to become a dangerous abdication of history."[8] This same criticism might also apply to post-racialism generally; indeed, in recent literature, the terms *post-black* and *post-racial* appear interchangeably.[9] Proponents of post-Blackness argue that it diverges from post-racialism in its acknowledgment of the importance of race while removing the determinism of collective racial identities. In the words of K. Merinda Simmons:

> Those who . . . critiqued claims of a populace that had enjoyed a 'post-race' environment since the election [of Barack Obama] seemed to have the answer. People of color did not have to live in a delusionary white fantasy of post-racialism. That was obviously an insulting proposition. Instead, [theorists] suggested that we begin thinking of a society that is clearly not post-racial but *is* just as clearly *post-black*.[10]

In this regard, post-Blackness scholars attempt to break out of the collectivism–individualism binary to offer a third concept that embraces individual Blacks in their individuality without negating the importance of race in society as a whole. This notion allows for collective understandings of socioeconomic standing without simultaneously implying a collective identity. Although the theory of post-Blackness may be a step in the right direction in terms of eradicating limiting conceptual binaries, it fails to acknowledge important ways in which collective action, and therefore Black socioeconomic progress, fundamentally rely on a sense of shared Black identity.

COLLECTIVE ACTION AND COMMON FATE

According to Stephen C. Wright, Donald M. Taylor, and Fathali M. Moghaddam, collective action is any action that aims to improve a group's conditions, such as status or power, and is enacted by a representative of the group.[11] Martijn van Zomeren, Tom Postmes, and Russell Spears identified three dominant sociopsychological perspectives explaining antecedent conditions for collective action: injustice, efficacy, and identity. Their chief supposition is that people are inclined to react to biased circumstances of disadvantage, which may or may not be the result of objective physical and social reality.[12] Michael Dawson; Patricia Gurin, Shirley Hatchett, and James S. Jackson; and Katherine Tate; all point to the role of racial oppression and class exploitation in stimulating Black collective action as a form of resistance to oppression and exploitation.[13] Many Black individuals view themselves as being disadvantaged similarly to other Blacks, which encourages collective action as a way to make socioeconomic gains.

Historically, one of the most important foundations of Black political belief was Blacks' perceived connection to other Blacks—that is, the extent to which Blacks believe that their fates as individuals are determined by what happens to Blacks as a group. Many political scientists who study Black political behavior believe that common fate results in political collective action by Blacks. The idea of common fate is a major component in understanding aspects of political cohesion among Blacks.[14]

The concept of common fate arose from psychologist Donald Campbell's attempt to clarify some of the perceived confusion in the way group theories were applied. Campbell focused on developing a theory to define "real" groups in the social world. He argued that a social entity identifiable as a real group should possess several properties in common. One of these was that a group must have individual elements that cluster together as a unit. Campbell considered this a general definition of common fate.[15]

Linked Fate in the 1980s: Michael Dawson and the National Black Election Panel Study

Linked fate is a specific theoretical version of the more general construct of common fate. Dawson described linked fate as: "based to a significant degree on the self-categorization and social identity theories of Turner and colleagues (1987). Individuals form their concepts of self at least in part by judging their similarity with and differences from others. . . . The key to understanding the self-categorization process for Blacks is the fact that *the social category 'black' in American society cuts across multiple boundaries.*"[16]

Gurin et al. and Tate related the idea of political interdependence or common fate to group issues. Tate introduced the concept early in her research and continued to use it as a feature of her "racial identification" measure. Gurin et al. noted that common fate and its relation to social identity had long been a feature of group theories. As early as 1948, Kurt Lewin wrote, "It is not similarity or dissimilarity of individuals that constitute a group, but interdependence of fate. Any normal group and certainly any developed and organized one, contains and should contain individuals of very different character."[17]

Similarly, Tate found that common fate perception was the strongest predictor of Blacks' attitudes regarding social services and race-specific programs. Blacks who scored high on common fate perception were more likely to support guaranteed jobs and minimum living standards, as well as to endorse greater government spending on "jobs for the unemployed, food stamps, and, to a lesser degree, Medicare."[18]

Michael Dawson's *Behind the Mule: Race and Class in African-American Politics* is a comprehensive exploration of linked fate. Dawson examines politically salient Black social cleavages using individual and collective Black political and public opinion data from the National Black Election Panel Study (NBES) of voting age adults from 1984 and 1988.[19] Linked fate in the 1984 and 1988 NBES was assessed by asking Black respondents if what happens to Blacks generally in the United States will be related to what happens to the respondents, personally. The survey also assessed Black attitudes about group economic subordination by asking whether Black respondents felt that the group's economic position relative to Whites overall was better, worse, or equal. Dawson's findings revealed that attitudes toward Black economic inferiority and linked fate were reciprocally reinforcing and that socioeconomic status weakly influences attitudes of linked fate. That is to say, socioeconomically diverse Blacks, despite their class differences, still identified with linked fate and attitudes of Black economic subordination.[20]

Dawson then used 1984 and 1988 NBES data to demonstrate the influence of linked fate in relation to Blacks' perceptions of costs versus benefits in relation to political party allegiance. Respondents were asked, "How hard do you think the Democratic/Republican Party really works on issues black people care about?"[21] Again, differences in attitudes based on socioeconomic status did not influence attitudes of cohesive political party allegiance.

Next, Dawson's NBES 1984 and 1988 data analysis examined the comparative influence of economics and racial group interests on Black political choice. The analysis examined presidential votes, support for Jesse Jackson, and evaluation of president Ronald Reagan. Additional analysis explored exit poll data for Blacks and Whites on support for Jesse Jackson in 1984 and 1988 in the primaries. Dawson found that, irrespective of individual socioeconomic status, Black racial group interests and economic status of Blacks in relation to Whites influenced Blacks' political choices.

Dawson also found that which Blacks perceive to be the racial interests and status of Blacks as a group directly predicted presidential approval ratings among individual Blacks. Examining Gallup presidential job approval ratings from 1961 to 1985, Dawson assessed Black and White differences in approval ratings in a variety of areas, including the racialized employment gap. The researcher found that the Black-White unemployment rate divide predicted Blacks' presidential approval. The larger the gap in racialized employment, the lower the president's approval rating among Blacks. It seems, however, that the predictive power of this divide was impeded by paradoxical ebullience, as Blacks consistently approved of President Obama, despite persistent economic stagnation.[22]

Despite the changing trends, linked fate remains intact among scholars because, as Dawson noted, it is rational to use group interests as a proxy for individual interests when more complete information is not available. Linked fate forms the core of the "Black Utility Heuristic," which posits that, as long as Blacks' chances in life are largely determined by race, it is logical that Blacks should use their "perceptions of the interest of African-Americans as a group, as a proxy for their own interest" in political decision-making.[23] According to this framework, when Blacks perceive that the group is doing well collectively, they perceive they are doing well individually, and therefore the sitting president is judged to be doing well.

Finally, Dawson examined more closely intra-group differences in policy preferences. Class divisions have been largely absent from historical analyses of race and from contemporary analyses of Black political choice, notwithstanding a diversity of political ideas among Blacks. Dawson hypothesized that class distinctions in Black political alignment had been overlooked because political surveys tend not to include questions important to the Black experience. The NBES data revealed that Blacks with high socioeconomic status (SES) favored fiscally conservative economic policies, as compared with those who were less financially well off, who preferred more redistributive economic policies. Respondents were asked, "How strongly do you approve or disapprove of a government guarantee of jobs or income?"[24] and whether they agreed with statements about Blacks forming an independent political party. Although high-SES Blacks were found to be more conservative than low-SES Blacks, Dawson found the gaps to be smaller between groups of Blacks than were gaps between Blacks and Whites.

As Dawson's important research shows, as recently as the 1980s, race remained a powerful influence on the public opinion of most Blacks, despite increased diversity and affluence in the Black class structure (upwardly mobile Blacks). Additionally, despite the divide that had been created between high- and low-SES Blacks, a linked-fate dynamic continued to exist connecting these subgroups of Blacks by unifying their political choices and party affiliations. Dawson noted that, as Blacks became more socioeconomically diverse, his results did not reflect a corresponding diversification of political opinion. For the past forty years, Blacks have voted for Democratic party candidates, irrespective of their social class.

Linked Fate in the 2010s: Christina Greer Examines Elevated Minority Status

In her study entitled *Black Ethnics: Race, Immigration, and the Pursuit of the American Dream*, Christina Greer highlighted the dynamics of coalition building versus competition between native-born Blacks and Black immigrants as it relates to attainment of the American Dream. She sought to answer the paradoxical question of why phenotypical Blacks (though immigrants) would, at times, not want to form coalitions with native-born Blacks in the light of what she called the "permanent black modifier" assigned to immigrant Blacks.[25]

Essentially, Greer found that immigrant Blacks view themselves through the lens of elevated minority status, contributing to this paradox. Though phenotypically Black and constrained by the predetermined boundaries of race, the dominant society attributes the American values of hard work and frugality to immigrant Blacks and highlights their educational attainment. In the dominant social view, immigrant Blacks should serve as an example to American-born Blacks, in the hope that the latter will stop making claims on American society for special favors.[26] For immigrant Blacks, this elevated status comes with a price. To be perceived as elevated and respected for possessing American values, they must intentionally remain "perpetual outsiders and forever foreign so as not to ever fully incorporate themselves into the Black American populace."[27]

Does the elevated minority model influence Black immigrants' public policy stances? And does it hinder Black immigrants from engaging in the political process and building coalitions with American-born Blacks? Through various national surveys and interviews with members of the New York City Social Service Employees Union Local 371, Greer found that the permanent Black modifier that attaches to Black immigrants in fact influences their political views more than their elevated minority status. Ethnic Africans were found to be the most optimistic about their socioeconomic prospects, while Afro-Caribbean and American-born Blacks were the most pessimistic about achieving the American Dream. American-born Blacks were also the most leery of forming coalitions with immigrant Blacks, particularly in the area of jobs.

Greer found that union membership (an example of linked fate leading to collective action) acted as a frame through which Black immigrants and American-born Blacks alike interpreted policy issues, such as government spending for socioeconomic policies that have implications for Blacks generally. Conversely, the less Blacks feel they belong to the group, the less likely it becomes that they will vote for policies that serve group interests. Given these phenomena, Blacks perceive that they must stick together if they are to advance.

Ultimately, differences in Black-White public opinion are greater than differences between Black groups. But Greer's findings on union membership and voting intention show that belonging to structural groups may be even more important in the development of group identity, especially political identity, today than it was in the 1980s. The crucial lesson to be taken from Dawson and Greer is that perceived linked fate is directly significant for Black politics. Therefore, such perceptions of linked fate may modulate the effect of paradoxical ebullience toward Black socioeconomic progress and prospects, implying that linked fate is necessary for cultivating collective action.

Black Politics as Common Fate/Collective Action

The Black struggle to achieve equal access to the political sphere and to gain influence over the political process was not viewed as an end in itself but rather as a way of empowering Blacks as a social group. As Martin Luther King Jr. wrote in 1965:

> Voting is the foundation stone for political action. With it the Negro can eventually vote out of office public officials who bar the doorway to decent housing, public safety, jobs and decent integrated education. It is now obvious that the basic elements so vital to Negro advancement can only be achieved by seeking redress from government at local, state, and federal levels. To do this, this vote is essential.[28]

Ironically, winning suffrage may have served to shift Blacks' political orientation from collectivism to individualism. Sociologists and political activists Frances Fox Piven and Richard Cloward stated that electoral politics restrain group politics.[29] That is, group consciousness can be undercut by the individualism inherent in the act of voting. (For example, the 2016 election of Donald Trump could be viewed as a victory of collectivization among right-wing activists, whereas the collectivism that elected Barack Obama was absent owing to the phenomenon of individualization after political victory; full analysis of such a possibility is outside the scope of the present work.) Moreover, suffrage may have undermined the perceived necessity of protest and collective action. Thus, despite the hope generated by the passing of the Voting Rights Act of 1965, Blacks' political gains may not have transformed socioeconomic conditions for Blacks at the lowest reaches of society.[30]

The promise of Black suffrage rests on two assumptions, both of which are faulty. One assumption was that the political process is in fact able to produce social change. On the contrary, history demonstrates that, although it is important to participate in the political process, politics is limited as an instrument of social change. Another assumption underlying Black focus on voting rights was that Blacks would remain politically cohesive and seek their common interests. This has not been the case.

There are opposing views of the Black political solidarity thesis. Historical and cultural sociologist Orlando Patterson, sociologist William Julius Wilson, and journalist Eugene Robinson, for example, argued that class is more significant than race as a way of understanding Blacks' chances in life or quality of life.[31] These authors questioned whether the increased diversity in Black opportunities for socioeconomic advancement would, over time, reduce Black collective action. Their argument connects to an important feature of the early literature of urban racial politics, which examined whether increasing diversity in the economic and social outcomes of ethnic groups eventually leads to changes in the nature of the group's politics. In the light of such studies, one must wonder whether Black attitudes in a putative post-racial America still embrace the idea of a collective struggle based on shared racial interests. Do Black political attitudes continue to reflect group interests, or are they now based on class needs or the concerns of individuals? Has the common pursuit of group interests among Blacks become nonexistent or perceived to be unnecessary because Blacks now view America as color-blind and post-racial? These questions are essential and will need to be addressed in due course.

Others who have studied the linked-fate phenomenon have come to similar conclusions regarding the influence of socioeconomic cleavages on linked fate among Blacks. For example, Tate found that educational attainment, age, political interest, and other cleavages, though present in Blacks, did not overpower the phenomenon of linked fate.[32] This echoes Christina Greer's finding that linked fate was present in political contexts irrespective of Blacks' ethnicity.

Based on these findings, it is clear that Blacks understand the impact of race on their life chances and outcomes. As a result, perceptions of linked fate remain high, even in this era of post-racial individualism and despite ever-changing political tides. This could be seen as a reorientation of Du Bois's notion of double consciousness; whereas, in Du Bois's time Blacks struggled to view themselves as both Americans and "Negros," today the challenge is the double consciousness of the self as both a member of a group and a self-sufficient individual.[33] The change, then, must be in the tools that Blacks use to attempt to achieve their collective goals, because it appears they already subscribe to the notion that their goals are collective. These collective goals cannot be achieved using individualist strategies. Ideologies such as color blindness, laissez-faire racism, and post-racialism have reoriented Blacks' views away from collective struggle toward an individualistic, self-sufficient posture; moreover, they have possibly contributed to paradoxical ebullience. The thesis of paradoxical ebullience argues that Blacks' understanding of Black group interests, including their worsening socioeconomic position, has shifted those interests from the collective to the individual, and the method to achieve those interests has shifted from protest politics to electoral politics. In addition, paradoxical ebullience supposes that these trends have political ramifications for Blacks that lead to negative economic consequences. In short, attitudes that are incongruent with Blacks' reality limit their collective political will to address their worsening economic position and jeopardize policies that provide economic benefits for Blacks.

CRITICAL RACE THEORY

Critical race theory (CRT) emerged out of critical legal studies, which found that racism was shaped by the U.S. legal system, specifically the legal categories that determine legal judgments. CRT aims to challenge color blindness by uncovering the intersectionalities and antiessentialist senses of racial identities. Proponents of CRT hold that "racism is endemic, institutional and systemic, a regenerative and overarching force maintaining all social constructs."[34]

Modern proponents of critical race theory adhere to *racial realism,* an attitude to race that pays special attention to tangible manifestations of racism and race-based power dynamics in society. Today's racial realism is a response to prior criticisms of CRT as an academic theory that failed to consider anything beyond the discursive aspects of race. According to racial realism, combatting racism requires one to acknowledge racism's real effects: discrimination, micro-aggressions, socioeconomic disparity, and disproportionate incarceration, among others. Instead of viewing discourse as the primary instrument of power in race relations, racial realism attributes primacy to power dynamics. Racial realism also involves alerting institutions of their routine false presentation of dominant cultural customs as universal.

Derrick Bell, the late Harvard Law Professor and a pioneer of CRT, noted that minority interests only have a chance of appearing in legislation when they converge with the interests of Whites. He called this the *interest-convergence principle.*[35] Indeed, most successful political efforts undertaken by minority communities over the past generation gained traction when their interests converged with those of Whites. For example, the civil rights movement succeeded in part because it shared Whites' fears. The leaders of the civil rights movement were able to merge concerns over the hypocrisy of the United States with the return of Black soldiers from World War II, and the transformation of the Southern economy from agricultural to industrial with White fears of communist aggression abroad and subversion at home. The interest-convergence principle is an offshoot of material-determinism, which posits that all changes in socially constructed ideas (such as race) result from economic incentives. We may also see here echoes of Hegel's historical theory of group difference as necessary and justified by world-historical progress; the communist "other" was a catalyzing factor in the civil rights movement, such that this new group difference might be seen as necessary in the light of the gains the movement made.

The paradoxical ebullience thesis holds that shifts in Black attitudes toward attaining social goals can be attributed to shifting social narratives or stories. Therefore, the CRT technique of *counter storytelling* should prove essential for overcoming resistance to collective action. Counter storytelling is rooted in perspectivism, the belief that one's specific standpoint influences how one sees truth. This conforms with a cultural view of race such as that proposed by Boas, Du Bois, and others who cited cultural circumstance as a determining factor in racial difference, such that the truth of racial divisions could change over time as collective perspectives change. In the context of CRT, scholars use counter storytelling to overcome the unexamined color blindness of majority institutions by reclaiming disenfranchised voices.[36] According to Richard Delgado and Jean Stefancic, "The voice-of-color thesis holds that because of their different histories and experiences with oppression, African American, Indian, Asian, and Latino/a writers and thinkers may be able to communicate [matters] to their White counterparts . . . that the Whites are unlikely to know."[37] The legal system tells its own story about the experience of race, but it often contradicts the lived experiences of minority individuals. In order to ensure accurate representation under the law, minority individuals must act to have their perspectives included in the official story. They may do this, for example, by comparing their personal narratives with legal narratives. In my analysis of paradoxical ebullience, I will use counter storytelling to examine the differences between the officially sanctioned "reality" and the experiences of the Black minority.

The above represents only a cursory glance at the basic tenets of CRT, but it should suffice to reveal CRT's purpose: to expose real racism in the modern world. But exposing and countering racism today requires a deeper understanding of how racism manifests itself in the contemporary color-blind era. Critical race theory stands in direct contradiction to the frames of color blindness. According to Kimberlé Williams Crenshaw, Neil Gotanda, Garry Peller, and Kendall Thomas, color blindness holds that the social category of race "is no longer in force."[38] Instead of adopting a color-blind attitude, CRT calls for a centrality and awareness of racial issues in legal discussions.

UNDERSTANDING COLOR-BLIND RACISM

Eduardo Bonilla-Silva identified four frames or themes in color-blind ideology: abstract liberalism, naturalization, cultural racism, and minimization. These themes constitute the manner in which, today, racial information is interpreted and racial attitudes are derived. A critical analysis of color-blind racism demonstrates the way its frames and their tenets covertly and overtly enable the abuse of power, the domination of minorities, and the perpetuation of socioeconomic inequality.

Abstract liberalism is the view that the civil rights movement of the 1960s caused a complete equalization of rights and opportunities for Blacks in the United States. Thus, abstract liberalism flatly denies that racial injustice exists with regard to education, employment, and other socioeconomic outcomes addressed by the Civil Rights Act. On this view, discrimination cannot be systemic but is rather a product of individual prejudices. Bonilla-Silva argued that abstract liberalism is the most important of the four frames because it promotes freedom for all, individualism, egalitarianism, and meliorism.

According to Bonilla-Silva, proponents of some forms of abstract liberalism believe that, with time, any residual effects of past prejudice will disappear on their own without intervention at any organizational level. As individual racism gradually dwindles away, the free market will eliminate racist effects via the laissez-faire effect. Therefore, these proponents hold, it is unnecessary to design laws and policies to combat racism. Abstract liberalism's supporters ask: How is it racist to be against policies that promote individualism? According to abstract liberalism, equal opportunity and freedom of choice, rather than preferential treatment and forced socioeconomic redistribution for disenfranchised Blacks, will lead to parity and optimal outcomes.[39]

Bonilla-Silva believes that abstract liberalism is a racist doctrine. In unimpeded and efficient market conditions, socially optimal outcomes might be achievable. As such, CRT's call for market intervention through social and economic policies, such as affirmative action and forced economic redistribution, could be viewed as racist. However, the paradox of abstract liberalism's call for an end to institutional racism is that it ignores the socioeconomic implications of slavery and Jim Crow on current Black socioeconomic status, as well as persistent White preferential treatment that excludes Blacks from economic participation.

Naturalization is the belief that racial inequality is natural. According to this view, racial inequality results from self-segregation of minority groups into distinct neighborhoods. Therefore, the inequality of residential outcomes, for example, between Blacks and Whites is a product of the free choice of racial groups rather than the result of segregationist social structures. Naturalization is a racist belief because it suggests that these segregationist "preferences" are essentially based in biology and typical of all societal groups, including Blacks.[40]

According to *cultural racism*, minority groups have adapted to being chronically underprivileged and socioeconomically unequal. This view originated in the late 1950s with Oscar

Lewis's theory of the culture of poverty. According to Lewis's theory, poor families adapt to the difficulties of poverty and develop value systems that allow them to survive and accept these abject conditions.[41] Cultural racism holds that these value systems perpetuate poverty by stifling social strategies for greater material success. The poor develop cultures of self-sabotaging attitudes and behaviors, which keep them from higher standards of living. Cultural racism is crucial to color-blind racism because it preserves the belief that racism plays no role in modern economic disparities; rather, the gap is the result of years of adaptation that no judicial change could possibly counteract.[42] Cultural racism is racist because it singles out Blacks as a group, making them alone responsible for their linked fate and for their outcomes, rather than engaging all Americans in working toward the value of equality.

Minimization, Bonilla-Silva's fourth and final theme, is the belief that racism may play an active role in determining social behavior, but its effect is so small that it merits no serious consideration. Furthermore, minimization implies that racial discrimination is no longer the primary dynamic influencing the life opportunities of minorities. Instead, the opportunities of minorities are determined by individual aptitudes and circumstances.

According to Bonilla-Silva, these four frames of color-blind racism have a small, indirect influence on Black racial attitudes. Color-blind ideology is, after all, the dominant explanation for stagnated Black socioeconomic progress, and to some extent Blacks are forced to use these frames, just as the majority uses them, to assess their own situations. However, the diverse racial attitudes of Blacks tend to attenuate the effect of the frames on some issues such as affirmative action, segregation, and education.

Each frame affects Black attitudes differently. Bonilla-Silva argued that Blacks primarily use the first three frames of color-blind racism to select information with which to compose their racial attitudes and to understand the conditions that prevent them from achieving their political and socioeconomic goals.

Cultural racism and naturalization have the strongest and most direct effects on Black racial attitudes. Additionally, these frames speak to personal lack or constraints in Blacks themselves. For example, Blacks use a narrative of cultural laziness to explain why they cannot achieve economic parity; they subscribe to the "culture of poverty." Following the doctrine of naturalization, Blacks also attribute racially disparate outcomes to natural differences or believe that disparate outcomes are natural. Blacks generally do not use abstract liberalism to articulate their racial attitudes; instead, they tend to believe that racial discrimination still dictates their life chances and socioeconomic outcomes. Accordingly, they also do not minimize the effects of racism in the United States.[43]

Bonilla-Silva highlighted color-blind racism's misrepresentation of the phenomenon of White hegemony, and its disingenuous representation of Black socioeconomic parity. While it is true Blacks have made some social and economic gains, color-blind racism obscures the fact that Blacks are still subject to structural racism and still lag substantially behind Whites.[44]

I return now to the questions posed at the beginning of this chapter. We have seen that color-blind racism and other contemporary post-racial concepts effectively discourage Blacks from believing that their fates are intertwined with the fate of other Blacks. Despite this growing sense of individualism, there is some evidence to suggest that race, rather than socioeconomic status or individual merit, systemically limits progress among Blacks in the United States. Post-racial ideology may seem empowering on an individual level, which largely explains its contemporary popularity. But such ideology runs the risk of disempowering Blacks as a group if the result is a decreased tendency to work together for structural equality. Despite the prominence of post-racial theory, Blacks still seem to view themselves as linked; it remains to be seen whether this view can translate to a desire to act collectively, rather than individually, to achieve common goals.

CHAPTER 2

Critical Discourse Analysis and Narratives of Race

n the next chapters, I employ critical discourse analysis to
identify the role of common fate, collective action, individualism, and ebullience in past and present narratives by Black
leaders to assess whether Black attitudes have indeed shifted
from collectivism to individualism and whether that shift (if
evident) has limited Black collective action to address deterio-
rating economic parity. The analysis also explores whether the
attitude shift in Blacks to a more optimistic, individualist bent
has detracted from Black collective action, and whether Blacks'
paradoxical ebullience threatens their socioeconomic progress.
In this chapter, I present the reader with a background of critical
discourse analysis as it relates to the study of race, and I discuss
the texts I have chosen to establish their appropriateness for this
type of analysis.

CRITICAL DISCOURSE ANALYSIS

Critical discourse analysis (CDA) examines the way written and
spoken words covertly and overtly support abuses of power,
dominations, and social inequalities. In addition, it formulates
ways in which speech and texts may resist such structures.
According to Teun van Dijk, a leading discourse analysis scholar,
CDA is intended to question existing conditions by identifying,
evaluating, repelling, and neutralizing representations of power

abuse as transmitted in private and public discourse.[1] CDA is committed to analysis of social wrongs such as prejudice and inequality in access to power, privilege, and symbolic resources. In order to achieve this goal, critical discourse analysts must be unequivocally conscious of their own roles in society— continuing a tradition that rejects the possibility of a "value free" science.[2] After all, as we have seen, the history of scientific and philosophical race discourse is everywhere laden with racial values and promotion of authors' self-interest. Critical discourse analysts maintain that science, and especially scholarly discourse, are inherently part of and influenced by social structures and produced in social interactions.[3] Using common themes such as power as a form of control, CDA involves examining, on micro and macro levels, the way discourse structures serve to reproduce patterns of social dominance regardless of the linguistic artifact that is being examined.

The *micro level* of analysis looks at the way people use language in spoken and written discourse, whereas the *macro level* examines the relationship between language and social power, dominance, and inequality between groups. For the purpose of this study, I will examine the speakers' use of liberalism, naturalization, cultural racism, and minimization at the micro level to influence Blacks' beliefs about their stagnated outcomes in ways that support macro-level power, dominance, and intergroup inequality.

There are several means of analyzing and connecting these levels. The first is to view language users as members of one or more social groups and interpret the speech of each group member as a group act. The second is to see such individual actions as part of group processes, such as reproducing sexism, writing legislation, or reporting news. Third, discursive interaction exists in the context of social structure and helps to constitute that structure, such that texts from within a given institution (e.g., the government) can be seen as part of that institution and its value system. Fourth, users of language are social actors who have individual memories, knowledge, and thoughts in addition to those that are shared with members of the group. Both individual and group thinking affect the interactions and discourse of individual members, while shared memories affect the group's collective actions.[4] These four tiers of analysis will help us to understand the complex relationships between elite Black discourses and the attitudes of individual Black social actors.

Power and Control

All forms of CDA revolve around the idea of *power*. Certain social groups have power if they are able to exert control over the acts and thoughts of the members of other groups in society. This ability to control individuals and groups though discourse requires that a privileged group has access to social resources such as coercion, wealth, social standing, fame, knowledge, information, or means of communication. The various kinds of power can be classified in terms of the resources used in their exercise. For example, military or criminal power is based solely on coercive force, whereas an economic elite may exercise power by expending financial and social capital. Further, power is generally relative, rather than absolute, so it is inherently unstable, provisional, and context-specific, making resistance possible.[5] For example, a general may be powerful within his military chain of command but subordinate to congressional oversight; an organized crime boss, while wealthy, may lack the social capital necessary to be influential in respectable circles; or the nonunionized factory worker may resist management domination by sabotaging equipment and stopping the production line. Following this line of reasoning, collective action by individual Blacks can be used to address the group's stagnated economic parity.

In order to analyze the relation between discourse and power, it is first necessary to identify ways in which access to particular forms of discourse constitutes a source of power. It may be possible to exert control over the actions of individuals through rhetoric or propaganda. Here, I draw on the research of van Dijk, Alessandro Duranti and Charles Goodwin, and Ruth Wodak to demonstrate the exertion of control over individuals through rhetoric.

I define power as control of or access to scarce resources. Because access to public discourse is a scarce resource, control of or access to it is also a form of power.[6] While people actively control everyday talk with people in their immediate social circles in private discourse, they only exert passive control over public discourse, which is actively controlled by more powerful groups. Further, those more powerful groups, be they employers, teachers, politicians, TV personalities, or CEOs of large corporations, aim their influence directly toward the less powerful and affect the beliefs and actions of people on lower strata by means of mass media. Accordingly, those with more influence over mass media, educational institutions and curricula, or the law have more influence over public discourse.[7]

It may be helpful to explain this distribution of power by citing an example from the U.S. legal system. Chief Justice John Roberts wrote for the majority in *Shelby County v. Holder*, stating that "our country has changed. . . . While any racial discrimination in voting is too much, congress must ensure that the legislation it passes to remedy that problem speaks to current conditions."[8] The legislation in question was the Voting Rights Act of 1965, which required that certain states with histories of Jim Crow discrimination submit to additional screenings during voting season to ensure that their polls did not impose restrictions to limit the minority vote. According to Chief Justice Roberts, the Voting Rights Act of 1965 was "based on 40-year-old facts having no logical relationship to the present day. Congress—if it is to divide the states—must identify those jurisdictions to be singled out on a basis that makes sense in light of current conditions, he wrote. It cannot simply rely on the past."[9] In this situation, Chief Justice Roberts, a person with the power to influence public discourse, denied the real threat of Jim Crow discrimination in the United States forty years after the passing of the Act, potentially contributing to continued inequality.

Control of Public Discourse

Within the framework of CDA, *discourse* is defined as a complex communicative act; individuals may exert power with the structure as well as the context of their text and speech. For the purposes of CDA, *context* consists of the mental representations of the social situation that relate to the production or understanding of discourse.[10] Context determines the way an issue is defined in relation to the specific time and place of the social situation, as well as communicative actions, participants' roles, and participants' mental representations. Therefore, the ability to control context is the ability to control one or more of these contextual categories. If, for example, an issue is publicly defined as one of minimization, where racism is not as bad as it used to be, people can be influenced to be ebullient despite socioeconomic realities. Furthermore, the way in which a question is framed can influence the response to that question. For example, a survey might ask whether affirmative action in school admission for Blacks is right or wrong but fail to mention preferential treatment for say, children of faculty or others to whom institutions might give preferential treatment. Such a survey might lead people to think that affirmative action is wrong because people should be admitted on their academic merit. If the survey question had framed the issue differently, responses might have differed.

According to Wodak, another critical aspect of control is the ability to structure speech and text, in other words, to speak and to write.[11] Members of powerful groups determine which forms of discourse are acceptable for less powerful groups to use. For example, suppose teachers have more power than their students. They may design tests with predetermined answers (multiple choice) or open answers (essay). This manifests their power over the ways in which their inferiors may communicate.

In the context of this study of Black attitudes toward economic stagnation, elites such as scholars, public officials, and researchers may (wittingly or not) structure the public discourse of Black socioeconomic stagnation by the way they frame issues of Black socioeconomic parity. By doing this, they control reports of Black ebullience.

Mind and Thought Control

Several features of communication allow the powerful to control the minds of the less powerful. The elite control influences not only the content of individuals' beliefs about the world but also the individuals' selection of sources to trust. Elites may use their power to limit alternative pubic discourses or media. Finally, members of marginalized groups may lack the understanding to resist the power of public discourse.[12] I argue here that elites use structural racism and social hierarchy to control Black ebullience regarding their current and future economic parity, relative to their actual economic parity.

As noted above, control that arises through discourse is based on people's understanding and representation of the text or speech and the time and place in which the communication occurs. In addition, the structures of discourse affect mental constructs with which people shape their ideas of what society should be. At a macro level, such structures define what people perceive as significant and correspond to their images of the ideal society. Likewise, rhetoric may be persuasive because of implied opinions that are taken for granted by the audience. Thus, a critical means of manipulating opinion is to communicate a belief without stating it explicitly, as this reduces the likelihood that it will be noticed and challenged.

All of these various features of public discourse provide opportunities for elite voices to shape Blacks' representations and expectations of mental and social ideals—essentially, to control their minds. When dominant groups, particularly elites, control the structure, content, and context of public discourse, they exert greater control over the public, especially over those who are marginalized. This control is not absolute because the inherent complexity and instability of communication and power renders the effects of public discourse unpredictable.[13] But it is clear that any understanding of public opinion must incorporate an analysis of both dominant and alternative discourses, which may influence public opinion, albeit sometimes without the public's explicit awareness.

BLACK STRUGGLE MOVEMENTS: RACE IN PUBLIC DISCURSIVE NARRATIVES

In an attempt to uncover the driving factors behind paradoxical ebullience, we must strive to understand how Black opinion has shifted, as we have seen, from collectivism to individualism. Critical discourse analysis allows us to view this shift from the perspective of messages delivered to the Black public by Black elites. In the discourses of the past, we will observe themes of common fate and collective action, emphasizing a need for Blacks to remain cohesive in order to advance both individual and group goals and maintain political and socioeconomic gains. We will also observe how these themes differ from the public discourse of today. Before we turn to individual texts that have informed Black attitudes, we must locate these texts historically through a survey of the key movements that characterize the history of racial attitudes in the United States, beginning with the Black Struggle movements of the mid-twentieth century.

The proponents of civil rights and Black Power during the 1950s and the 1960s treated common fate and collective action as prerequisite for the building of Black communities as well as the achievement of their political and socioeconomic goals. These narratives presented Blacks with a twofold charge: on the one hand, to work together on behalf of all Blacks through the justice system to achieve equality and parity with Whites, on the other, to throw off the shackles of racism and inequality by any means necessary.

Broadly speaking, the struggle of Blacks in the United States has manifested itself in three ways: cultural nationalism, revolutionary nationalism, and the civil rights movement. All three of these Black emancipatory movements arose out of the Black experience of political, social, and economic oppression. Although each movement is distinct from and opposed to the others in many cases, all three share Black emancipation as their primary goal. Specifically, they strove to achieve racial equality for Blacks by removing the obstacles to Black success put in place by White-dominated society. To varying degrees, these three approaches also aimed to preserve Black identity as distinct from White identity.[14] Despite their common goals, the Black Struggle movements adopted widely varying approaches of working toward Black socioeconomic parity. In the paragraphs that follow, I discuss the approaches of these three movements in detail, drawing on the work of Marcus Garvey on cultural nationalism, Malcolm X and Stokely Carmichael[15] for revolutionary nationalism, and Martin Luther King Jr. for the civil rights movement. These speakers had in common a goal of uplifting Blacks politically and socioeconomically as well as creating a sense of Black unity and pride.

Cultural Nationalism

In "Facing the Challenges of a New Age," Martin Luther King Jr. said of Marcus Garvey: "Garvey was the first man of color in the history of the United States to lead and develop a mass movement. He was the first man on a mass scale and level to give millions of Negroes a sense of dignity and destiny, and make the Negro feel he is somebody."[16]

Marcus Garvey's cultural nationalism focused on maintaining a specifically Black identity through the creation of Black American culture. He emphasized Black value and identity and viewed White-dominated cultural traditions, including those of music and literature, as hegemonic. African diaspora historians John H. Bracey, August Meier, and Elliott Rudwick state that the era "from about 1880 to 1930 witnessed the flowering of a clear-cut cultural nationalism. It was evident particularly in a rising self-conscious interest in the race's past and in efforts to stimulate a distinctively black literature."[17] The New Negro movement was one manifestation of Black cultural nationalism seeking to promote self-motivation and ethnic pride among Blacks.[18]

Within Black cultural nationalism, it is possible to distinguish three primary cultural movements: Garveyism, the Harlem Renaissance, and Pan-Africanism.[19] Each of these movements aimed generally to develop a sense of connection between Black Americans and their African heritage. Toward this end, the movements embraced African culture by emphasizing the ways in which Black American culture derives from it. This gave specificity to Black cultural nationalism, which allowed it to resonate with a broader audience of Black Americans. The Harlem Renaissance was characterized by the adoption of African elements in art, which further strengthened the link between Africa and Black Americans.[20] These movements largely succeeded in developing and strengthening Black group identity. In the words of Dr. King, Garveyism "attained mass dimensions, and released a powerful emotional response because it touched a truth which had long been dormant in the mind of the Negro. There was reason to be proud of their heritage as well as of their bitterly won achievement in America."[21]

Revolutionary Nationalism

Revolutionary nationalism, also called militant nationalism, can be described as a stronger form of cultural nationalism with an emphasis on complete separation of Blacks from Whites. Its genesis was influenced by the assassination of civil rights leaders as well as organizations such as the Nation of Islam.

The militant organizations of revolutionary nationalism differed from the cultural nationalism movement primarily in their contempt for integration. The Nation of Islam, for example, arose in the 1930s as a religious and political movement. Unlike the organizations associated with the civil rights movement, the Nation of Islam emphasized the separation between White-dominated society and Black American culture. The movement's leaders argued that equality was not possible through integration. According to Manning Marable, revolutionary nationalists systematically opposed White institutions while supporting all Black institutions. They wanted "complete freedom, justice and equality, or recognition and respect as human beings."[22] Other militant groups, including the Student Nonviolent Coordinating Committee (SNCC), sought fundamental change in the existing social and economic structures so that Black Americans could be in control of their own society, economy, culture, and politics.[23] They believed that the successes of the civil rights movement were not enough, that they benefited only the elite, and that the majority of Blacks were still oppressed by the status quo.

Two other manifestations of revolutionary nationalism were the Republic of New Africa and the Black Panther Party. The Republic of New Africa, formed in 1967, hoped to create a black nation independent of the United States. The New Africa would be located in the American South. Supporters of this idea were prepared to engage in physical combat to attain their objectives. The Black Panther Party, in 1966, developed one of the most detailed plans for fundamental structural change, a ten-point program. Among the ten points advocated by the Black Panther Party were self-determination, education, housing, social justice, and political power.[24]

The violent nature of revolutionary nationalism caused difficulties for these movements between 1964 and 1972. In response to urban rebellions that took place in Black communities, leaders of the movements were routinely imprisoned, forced into exile, or killed.

Civil Disobedience and the Civil Rights Movement

The nonviolent civil disobedience political-resistance movement complemented themes of unity in Black cultural nationalism. According to Anthony Smith, group identity is composed of "both a cultural and political identity and is located in a political community as well as a cultural one."[25] It may be argued that Black cultural nationalism's emphasis on Black unity would not have been effective without the efforts of the nonviolent civil disobedience movement to mobilize Blacks politically. The civil rights movement provided this political mobilization, and, at the same time, it is possible that it would not have succeeded without the strong sense of Black unity that had developed in the mid-twentieth century.[26]

The civil rights movement began as an articulation, in political language, of the problems that Black cultural nationalism had been attempting to address. Organizing around this articulation allowed the Black community to gather the resources necessary to stage political interventions and collective actions that aimed at creating structural change. An important aspect of this organization was the mobilization of individuals within Black communities—a micro-level mobilization. As Doug McAdam, John D. McCarthy, and Mayer N. Zald explain, mobilizing individuals on a micro level (locally) is as crucial an element in creating structural change as mobilization at a macro level (nationally).[27] The urban migration of Blacks, as well as the new political language adopted by the civil rights movement, enabled this micro-level mobilization in the urban South.

Mobilization of Blacks took place largely under the auspices of organizations like the NAACP and the Congress of Racial Equality (CORE). These organizations were among the first to stimulate political changes that would bring about racial equality for Black Americans. During the 1940s and 1950s, many of these organizations' efforts were strongly opposed by the existing White-dominated political order. This opposition led civil rights leaders such as Martin Luther King Jr. to declare:

"Freedom is never voluntarily given by the oppressor; it must be demanded by the oppressed."[28] In this and similar statements, King helped to define the new political language that would inform and guide the civil rights movement. King's statements constituted discursive structures that leaders of that time used to shape Black attitudes toward normative values of equality and to remind Blacks that reality and rhetoric about socioeconomic parity did not agree. In addition to their attempts to create change from within existing political and legal systems, the organizations involved in the civil rights movement, including CORE, began to protest and organize nonviolent direct action.[29]

During the 1950s and 1960s, the civil rights movement spread and spawned new organizations such as the Southern Christian Leadership Conference (SCLC) and SNCC.[30] These new organizations joined CORE and the NAACP to promote nonviolent protest and to agitate for change. Increased organization convinced Americans that organizations like the SCLC were rallying points of a broad-based movement. These groups attracted talented individuals who were interested in using their skills and resources in service of the civil rights movement.

Martin Luther King Jr. was one such individual. He joined the SCLC and became the unofficial leader of the movement. As a Christian leader, King emphasized "moral and spiritual life" in his rhetoric and exposed contradictions between Christian values and the segregation and oppression of Blacks.[31] He believed that the civil rights movement extended beyond racial issues to other forms of social and economic inequality, which characterized this movement as integrationist. In addition to racism, King identified economic exploitation and war as primary social evils.[32] Although the civil rights movement enjoyed some success in the form of the passage of the Civil Rights Act of 1964 and other civil rights laws, King recognized that the struggle for broad social equality was far from over. Marable suggested that King's refusal to stop supporting and working toward "radical reforms in America" might have contributed to his assassination in 1968.[33] Similarly, Robert Allen suggests that both King and Malcolm X were assassinated "at precisely the point at which they began working actively and consciously against the racism and exploitation generated by the American capitalist system."[34] In other words, these leaders were interested in identifying ways in which existing political, economic, and social structures were inherently flawed and unable to bring about the type of change that the civil rights movement hoped to accomplish. The assassinations of King and Malcolm X had a profound effect on the Black community in that they increased support for militant resistance in the Black Struggle movement. The end of the civil rights movement coincided with a drastic decline in discussions of racism, to the point that America was already said to be post-racial.

Post-Racial Narratives and Black Socioeconomic Parity

Present-day post-racial narratives from prominent Blacks like former President Barack Obama counsel Blacks to stop complaining about the past. Leaders say that conditions are much better now in terms of the oppressive burdens of discrimination. Indeed, the Obama presidency coincided with the Black ebullient boom, and most of the discussion about America entering a post-racial era has centered on his 2008 election. Not only has Obama's presidency had unprecedented effects on Black attitudes, but Obama also stands among the powerful Black elite who have produced public discourse on how Blacks interact with society, how they should interact with society, and the likely outcomes of their hard work and responsible behavior. As a Black elite instructing Black masses from an unprecedented position of Black power, Obama's speeches will be crucial to this analysis of paradoxical ebullience.

Linguist and public intellectual John McWhorter, in his works *Losing the Race: Self Sabotage in Black America* and *Winning the Race: Beyond Crisis in Black America,* blames Blacks for their stagnated socioeconomic outcomes. He attributes their stagnation to a culture of victimhood, dependency, and alienation that arose during the civil rights era. The post-racial message to Blacks is this: work harder and be more responsible and you, too, can achieve the American Dream. McWhorter has produced abundant discourse on Blacks' interactions with society and how they perceive the world. His studies culminated in an explanation of Blacks' socioeconomic stagnation that is consistent with a post-racialist frame: Blacks refuse to work hard and be responsible, so they suffer economically. McWhorter's discourse is ebulliently prescriptive in that he laid out a plan to get Black socioeconomics progressing again, including new Black leadership.

Andra Gillespie, in *Whose Black Politics?: Cases in Post-Racial Black Leadership,* and Fredrick C. Harris, in *The Price of the Ticket: Barack Obama and the Rise and Decline of Black Politics,* examined the impact of such ebulliently prescriptive, bootstrap messages on Blacks, specifically in terms of the ability of the messages to advance political and socioeconomic agendas, making them natural inclusions in a critical discourse analysis related to Black political opinions and actions. Gillespie's work described the deracialized approach to governance and policy among emerging Black leadership. Harris has espoused a narrative that demonstrates how the election of Barack Obama as the nation's first Black president was simultaneously a defining moment for the United States and a moment signaling what may very well be the end of common fate and collective action as strategies for achieving political and socioeconomic parity for Blacks.

For my critical discourse analysis of themes of common fate, collective action, ebullience, and individualism in the post-racial era, I will focus on texts from these authors. I have deliberately included narratives from speakers on both the right and left sides of the political spectrum, as well as Black scholars who have written Black political leadership discourse. Each narrative brings a distinct perspective to my study.

The critical discourse analysis method is not without limitations in assessing the impact of these discursive trends on Black attitudes and behaviors. Virtually all social science research uses methods that limit and direct research findings to some degree. One limitation of the critical discourse method is that it does not allow for causal relationships to be drawn between Black racial attitudes and socioeconomic outcomes as influenced by post-racial discourse. However, we will find that the analysis reveals patterns that may inform policy and social behavior in significant ways.

CHAPTER 3

Ebullience and Action in Black Discourse

I n this chapter, I draw on critical race theory (CRT) and critical discourse to analyze themes of collective action, common fate, and individualism in civil rights, Black Power, and post-racial narratives. My goal is to assess qualitatively the attitudinal trends of Blacks in both eras as they relate to Black ebullience about Black socioeconomic parity and policy preferences. The ultimate aim is to determine whether Black ebullience diminishes Black collective action that is meant to address Black stagnated socioeconomic parity, especially as it relates to Blacks' disposition to lobby for policies that provide them with socioeconomic benefits.

OUTLINE OF THE ANALYSIS

Martin Luther King Jr., Malcolm X, and Stokely Carmichael are recognized leaders of the civil rights and Black Power movements. Their texts span from the late 1950s to the late 1960s, and I intend to use them as a cross section of civil rights and Black Power narratives to assess Black attitudinal trends during these eras. King's speeches, "A Realistic Look at the Question of Progress in the Area of Race Relations," "Give Us the Ballot," "The Other America," and "I've Been to the Mountain Top," relate to the question of whether Black ebullience diminishes a sense of common fate among Blacks and, consequently, the ability of Blacks to work collectively to advance their socioeconomic standing. "A Realistic Look at the Question of Progress" discusses race relations, Black socioeconomic status, and ebullience, all of which directly concern this analysis. "Give Us the Ballot" and "The Other America" also discuss notions of common fate and collective action as the means to improve Black socioeconomic parity. Two of Malcolm X's speeches, "The Ballot or the Bullet" and his speech at Ford Auditorium, stand out for their emphasis on the common experience of oppression that all Blacks face and for the importance that Malcolm X placed on the need for collective action to overcome this oppression. Finally, Stokely Carmichael's "Black Power" addresses common fate, shared oppression, and the need for collective action to counter a long history of organized Black oppression. Additionally, "Black Power" includes a rich discussion of Black diligence alongside Black indifference. I chose the aforementioned speeches to give a diverse picture of elite Black sentiments toward Black socioeconomic parity.

I begin my thematic analysis of post-racial narratives with McWhorter's *Losing the Race: Self-Sabotage in Black America* and *Winning the Race: Beyond the Crisis in Black America* in which he states that Black negativity stunts Black achievement. Because McWhorter is a linguist, rather than a race scholar per se, he is often less well known in academic race circles than some of the other elites included here. However, he is a popular public intellectual whose writing has appeared regularly in a wide range of outlets (such as the *Wall Street Journal* and the *New Republic*), which makes him a particularly prominent voice on race issues among the educated Black public where he is more well known. He has also contributed to recent policy in his capacity as a fellow of at least one conservative think tank. I then proceed to analyze Andra Gillespie's *Whose Black Politics?: Cases in Post-Racial Black Leadership*, which frames the emergence of new Black leadership and its deracialized approach to governance and policy. Then I move on to President Obama's commencement speeches to Morehouse College (2013) and Barnard College (2012), as well as his address at the 99th Annual Convention of the National Association for the Advancement of Colored People (NAACP) in 2008. The Morehouse and NAACP speeches are directly concerned with the tension between behavioral and structural explanations of Black socioeconomic stagnation. To broaden the analysis outside the context of speeches to Blacks, I opted to include Obama's speech to Barnard. This speech provided a parallel with the Morehouse commencement address, but with a very different audience. Although these speeches are not intended as a comprehensive summary of Obama's discourse on Black socioeconomic progress or collective action, they provide enough of a range to support some conclusions about the nature of his discourse generally. Additionally, their temporal location before or in the early years of the presidency narrow the analysis to rhetorical trends that would have had time to take effect in the minds of the Black public by the end of the Obama presidency. I contrast Obama's texts against one another as well as against the texts of Gillespie and McWhorter. Finally, I discuss the paradoxical effects of Obama's election on Black power, as described by Fredrick Harris. These texts will fuel a later discussion of self-help as it relates to Black power and paradoxical ebullience.

Despite the careful consideration given to the selection of texts to include a range of views and avoid "cherry picking," it is worth noting that any such selection is bound to limit the scope of the analysis to some extent. All the speakers included here were or are prolific, and volumes would have to be written to analyze their full bodies of discourse. Nevertheless, my hope is that the analysis provided here will lead to a deeper understanding of the phenomenon of paradoxical ebullience. Future research can be conducted to identify confirmation or disconfirmation of this understanding elsewhere.

MARTIN LUTHER KING JR.: POOLING INDIVIDUAL CAPITAL TO PROMOTE COLLECTIVE GAIN

The Question of Progress

Black common fate and collective action feature prominently in King's narratives. In "A Realistic Look at the Question of Progress in the Area of Race Relations" (King's address in St. Louis), he said that individuals residing in states that were adopting integration "have the moral responsibility to use the ballot and use it well. Yes, we must continue to gain the ballot. . . . People in the North ask me from time to time, 'What can we do to help in the South?' Get the ballot and through gaining the ballot you gain political power. And you can call the politicians and tell them that certain things will have to be done because you helped put them in office."[1]

Although King's call for the ballot attributed great power to the individual vote, he intended for Blacks to use their individual votes to ameliorate socioeconomic conditions for Blacks as a group. King's call was not only meant to be a charge of self-help in terms of attitudes, customs, and norms of hard work and social responsibility, but also a call to use individual power to dismantle the discriminatory structural institutions and policies that marginalized Blacks as a group. Thus, King simultaneously promoted individualistic and collectivist values. Tellingly, however, King would later come to regard this emphasis on voting (an individualistic action), as opposed to collective economic enfranchisement, as a mistake of the civil rights movement.

Among King's most overtly collectivist messages was his call, in the same 1957 address, for individual Blacks to contribute their funds to "go down in our pockets and give big money for the cause of freedom . . . We have a long, long way to go and we are going to have to spend a lot of money to get there."[2] He continued, "If we are going to get it, we are going to have to work for it, and we are going to have to give our money for it."[3] "Our money," for King, meant "Black money." Imploring Blacks to unite for freedom and equality, King urged their continued financial support of the NAACP because it "has done more to achieve the civil rights of Negroes over any other organization."[4] Again, King envisioned the use of individual capital to promote a collective end.

In King's work we find echoes of the key themes of CRT. For example, King recognized abstract liberalism as a tenet of color-blind racism that promotes individualism. In his time the rights of the individual did not exist for Blacks. Accordingly, King reminded Blacks that, although some progress was made regarding policies on race relations, the fate of individual Blacks was tied to the fate of Blacks as a group as they appeared under the law. Consistent with the racial realism of CRT, King confronted the evidence of racism. He reminded Blacks that power lies in access to the ballot as a way to influence the distribution of scarce resources.

"Give Us the Ballot"

King's strongest calls for collective action and emphasis on common fate come from "A Realistic Look at the Question of Progress," where he called on "every freedom-loving Negro, from all over the nation . . . to come to Washington."[5] He intended to "appeal to the conscience of the nation to do something . . . to carry the civil rights bill."[6] King furthered this call in his "Give Us the Ballot" speech, in which he claims the fate of the individual Black depends on the fate of the group.[7] In this instance, the fate of the Black vote was tied to each Black individual's right to vote. King highlighted the "conniving methods" being used "to prevent Negroes from becoming registered voters."[8] He initiated an inspiring call for increased protection of the Southern Negroes' right to the ballot:

> Give us the ballot, and we will no longer have to worry the federal government about our basic rights. Give us the ballot, and we will no longer plead to the federal government for passage of an anti-lynching law; we will by the power of our vote write the law on the statute books of the South and bring an end to the dastardly acts of the hooded perpetrators of violence.

Give us the ballot, and we will transform the salient misdeeds of bloodthirsty mobs into the calculated good deeds of orderly citizens. Give us the ballot, and we will fill our legislative halls with men of goodwill and send to the sacred halls of Congress men who will not sign a "Southern Manifesto" because of their devotion to the manifesto of justice. Give us the ballot, and we will place judges on the benches of the South who will do justly and love mercy, and we will place at the head of the southern states governors who will, who have felt not only the tang of the human, but the glow of the Divine. Give us the ballot, and we will quietly and nonviolently, without rancor or bitterness, implement the Supreme Court's decision of May seventeenth, 1954.[9]

After his call for the Black vote, King rallied for collective action from Black leaders, the federal government, White Northern liberals, and White moderate Southerners to make racial justice a reality.

King's "Give Us the Ballot" speech is consistent with CRT in that it highlights the "conniving methods" used to stymie Blacks' access to the ballot. These conniving methods, to King, were evidence of racism. King's appeal to the nation's moral consciousness echoes CRT's goal of bringing awareness to routine discrimination as Eurocentric in nature (something that Whites do when they colonize non-White peoples). These influential speeches, rooted in perspectivism, highlight Blacks' marginalized position and invite them to weigh in on the discrimination they experience. By contrast, adherents of color-blind ideologies would view the marginalized position of Blacks as a naturally occurring outcome, the result of Blacks' pathological values and culture, or even as a biological difference (reminding us of Thomas Jefferson's position), not racism. This shows that King's speeches are diametrically opposed to the frames of color-blind racism.

"The Other America"

"The Other America," King's March 14, 1968, speech, primarily highlighted Black common fate and how opportunity and outcomes for Blacks are based on race and collective action as a means to achieve group gains that translate to individual gains.[10] Four years after the Civil Rights Act of 1964 and three years after the Voting Rights Act of 1965, King's focus turned to economic inequality and unfulfilled Black freedom and justice. King highlighted the role of race in these phenomena:

> Thousands and thousands of people, men in particular walk the streets in search for jobs that do not exist. In this other America, millions of people are forced to live in vermin-filled, distressing housing conditions where they do not have the privilege of having wall-to-wall carpeting, but all too often, they end up with wall-to-wall rats and roaches. Almost forty percent of the Negro families of America live in substandard housing conditions. In this other America, thousands of young people are deprived of an opportunity to get an adequate education. . . . Probably the most critical problem in the other America is the economic problem. There are so many other people in the other America who can never make ends meet because their incomes are far too low if they have incomes, and their jobs are so devoid of quality. And so, in this other America, unemployment is a reality and underemployment is a reality.[11]

King spurred Blacks to collective action, stating, "*We* must always work with an effective, powerful weapon and method that brings about tangible results."[12] Here he used militant imagery to represent a massive, non-violent collective action that would combat policies of structural socioeconomic inequalities. King condemned America for ignoring "the plight of the negro poor."[13]

In order to solve the problem of Blacks in poverty, King countered four myths. First, in line with CRT's racial realism, America must collectively recognize that the country is still racist and racism has to be done away with. Additionally, King critiqued the abstract liberal frame that racial injustice no longer existed because civil rights effected a complete equalization of Black rights and opportunities. Second, King argued that the myth that time will solve the problem of racial injustice must be discarded, and that the color-blind frame of minimization, claiming that conditions for Blacks are better presently than in the past, were false.

> Somewhere, we must come to see that human progress never rolls in on the wheels of inevitability, it comes through the tireless efforts and the persistent work . . . without this hard work, time itself becomes an ally of the primitive forces of social stagnation.[14]

King recognized the role of dismantling power relations and hierarchies, and the social transformation of the position of Blacks checks color-blind racism's minimization frame. He admonished Blacks that progress happens through deliberate and persistent efforts of political activism: "We must always help time and realize that the time is always right to do right."[15] The changes proposed by Blacks through political activism would ultimately align with the interest of Whites to then bring about equality for marginalized Blacks. This echoes CRT-scholar Derrick Bell's interest-convergence principle. Third, King believed the myth that legislation is not the way to solve the problem of racial injustice needed to be silenced, and that lawmakers needed to be pressed into action and that the laws needed to be enforced. He argued: "It may be true that morality cannot be legislated, but behavior can be regulated. It may be true that the law cannot change the heart but it can restrain the heartless. It may be true that the law can't make a man love me, but it can restrain him from lynching me."[16]

The fourth and final myth King dispelled was the bootstrap philosophy, according to which Black individuals should be allowed to fail or succeed on their own merits. The "tireless efforts and persistent work" to which King referred were collective in nature because they were designed to indicate the role of racial oppression and exploitation in stimulating Black collective action to improve Black socioeconomic conditions.

King fully supported Blacks as individuals engaging in self-help and doing what they could to better themselves economically, but this was only part of the picture for him. Again, though nuanced with individualistic calls for Blacks to do what they could for themselves, King's calls for action were directed toward racially discriminatory institutions and systems. "No ethnic group," King said, "has completely lifted itself by its own bootstraps."[17] He went on to point out that, while America did not make good on its promise to endow Blacks with forty acres and a mule so they could "get started in life," Congress gave millions of acres in land grants in the West and Midwest, built land grant colleges, and provided low interest rates for farm equipment to White farmers, who subsequently received millions in federal subsidies to not farm. Ironically, these people were preaching bootstrap philosophy to Blacks.[18]

King encouraged Blacks in collective action, saying the alternative to "riots on the one hand and timid supplication for justice on the other" was "militant massive non-violence."[19] When President Johnson told King that he would not be able to get a Black voting rights bill through Congress, the Selma voting rights movement was organized in Alabama, and, shortly afterward, the Voting Rights Act was passed. Referencing the Selma movement and the passage of the Voting Rights Act, King declared, "Things don't happen until the issue is dramatized in a massive direct-action way."[20] King used a narrative strategy of dramatization to portray the plight of "The Other America—America's Negros" and generate support for collective action.

King delivered his final speech, "I've Been to the Mountaintop," four years after the passage of the Civil Rights Act and three years after Black enfranchisement.[21] It was an address in support of striking sanitation workers in Memphis. Like his other speeches, this speech calls for unity, nonviolence, protests, and boycotts. King again denied abstract liberalism and promoted Black unity. He reminded the gathered audience: "Individually, we are poor. . . . Never stop and forget that collectively—that means all of us together—collectively we are richer than all of the nations in the world, with the exception of nine. . . . That's power right there, if we know how to pool it."[22]

King asked listeners to "be concerned about your brother. . . . You may not be on strike. . . . But either we go up together, or we go down together."[23] Referencing the Hebrews in captivity under Pharaoh, King said, "When the slaves get together, that's the beginning of getting out of slavery."[24] This comparison bespeaks King's racial realism. By equating slavery to the inequality experienced by Blacks due to discrimination, King acknowledged the intractability of racism. The agenda called for economic sanctions against companies who were discriminatory in their hiring policies. Those who were able to were also called on to support the needs of the striking sanitation workers. King's realism echoed that of Jesse Jackson: "Up to now, only the garbage men have been feeling the pain; now we must kind of redistribute the pain."[25]

Martin Luther King Jr. on Ebullience

As we saw in an earlier chapter, optimism is the belief that good outcomes will result from little or no intervention. Ebullience, then, is the extreme optimism exhibited by Blacks about their socioeconomic position relative to their socioeconomic reality. In his speech "A Realistic Look at the Question of Progress in the Area of Race Relations," King stated there are three fundamental attitudes toward racial progress. The first, which is my focus here, is extreme optimism; the second is extreme pessimism; and the third is the realistic position. King cautioned against extreme optimism, stating that the extreme optimist would conclude, based on the strides of civil rights, "that the problem is just about solved, and that we can sit comfortably by the wayside and wait on the coming of the inevitable."[26] The optimist would, as King states, "point proudly to the marvelous strides that have been made in the area of civil rights over the last few decades."[27] In short, extreme optimism leads to complacency and the belief that there is no longer any need to act collectively, protest, or call attention to the vestiges of racism, because they will soon be gone.

Similarly, in "Give Us the Ballot," King cautioned Blacks against extreme optimism. He called on Blacks to be prudent and not to succumb to the temptation of "being victimized with the psychology of victors."[28] He went on to remind Blacks that, despite victories, "we must not . . . remain satisfied with a court victory over our white brothers. We must respond to every decision with an understanding of those who have opposed us and with an appreciation of the difficult adjustments that the court orders pose for them. We must act in such a way as to make possible a coming together of white people and colored people on the basis of a real harmony of interest and understanding. We must seek an integration based on mutual respect."[29]

Along these same lines, in his speech "I've Been to the Mountaintop," King told his supporters of the need to keep the issue of injustice in focus and to "force everybody to see that there are thirteen hundred of God's children here suffering, sometimes going hungry, going through dark and dreary nights, wondering how this thing is to come out."[30] In all of these speeches, King does two things: he counters the complacency of extreme optimism by emphasizing racial realism and the need for continued struggle, and he fosters collective action by addressing Black people in the first-person plural.

Given these trends in King's discourse, it is highly likely that, if he were speaking to Blacks today, he would caution them against taking an ebullient attitude toward their socioeconomic progress, especially in light of the contradictory socioeconomic data. Perhaps King would say that this attitude of extreme optimism may make Blacks feel as if the battle is already won and thus hinder the collective action necessary to producing meaningful social change.

MALCOLM X: SUBMERGING DIFFERENCE IN THE PURSUIT OF COLLECTIVE EMANCIPATION

"The Ballot or the Bullet"

In his address entitled "The Ballot or the Bullet," Malcolm X emphasized the common experience of oppression faced by all Blacks, irrespective of their religious beliefs. This is consistent with the idea of common fate as described by Dawson; Gurin, Hatchett, and Jackson; and Tate. In contrast to how he is sometimes popularly portrayed, Malcolm X agreed with King: despite new legislation, Blacks were still not equal to Whites under the law. Malcolm X pioneered Black empowerment across every socioeconomic class, revealing himself as a staunch racial realist:

> It's time for us to submerge our differences and realize that it is best for us to first see that we have the same problem, a common problem, a problem that will make you catch hell whether you're a Baptist, or a Methodist, or a Muslim, or a nationalist. Whether you're educated or illiterate, whether you live on the boulevard or in the alley, you're going to catch hell just like I am. We're all in the same boat and we all are going to catch the same hell from the same man. He just happens to be a white man. All of us have suffered here, in this country, political oppression at the hands of the white man, economic exploitation at the hands of the white man, and social degradation at the hands of the white man. Now in speaking like this, it doesn't mean that we're anti-white, but it does mean we're anti-exploitation, we're anti-degradation, we're anti-oppression. And if the white man doesn't want us to be anti-him, let him stop oppressing and exploiting and degrading us. Whether we are Christians or Muslims or nationalists or agnostics or atheists, we must first learn to forget our differences. If we have differences, let us differ in the closet; when we come out in front, let us not have anything to argue about until we get finished arguing with the man.[31]

This call to set aside religious differences and unite for the sake of equality acknowledges the power of the Black voting bloc. In theory, if Blacks unified as a voting bloc, they could use their pooled political power to swing the election toward candidates who would promote Black issues. On the power of the collective action of Black voters, Malcolm X explained: "When white people are evenly divided, and black people have a bloc of votes of their own, it is left up to [Black people] to determine who's going to sit in the White House and who's going to be in the dog house."[32]

Here, Malcolm X foreshadowed Derrick Bell's interest-convergence principle by holding Blacks accountable for their economic goals. Reprimanding Blacks for their misuse of the ballot in the previous election and coaching them on how to wield the collective power of the Black vote in the upcoming election of 1964, Malcolm X admonished:

> It was the black man's vote that put the present administration in Washington, D.C.[33] Your vote, your dumb vote, your ignorant vote, your wasted vote put in an administration in Washington, D.C., that has seen fit to pass every kind of legislation imaginable, saving you until last, then filibustering on top of that. So it's time in 1964 to wake up. And when you see them coming up with that kind of conspiracy, let them know your eyes are open. And let them know you—something else that's wide open too. It's got to be the ballot or the bullet. A ballot is like a bullet. You don't throw your ballots until you see a target, and if that target is not within your reach, keep your ballot in your pocket.[34]

Here we clearly see Malcolm X, a Black elite leader, blaming Blacks as a group for the state of American politics in the early 1960s.

Ford Auditorium, 1965

In his speech at Ford Auditorium, Malcolm X contrasted the commitment to justice among Black Americans with the attitude of the indigenous Africans he met when he traveled to the African continent.[35] He was struck by the fervor with which African Blacks organized, worked, and pressured their colonizers to stop the injustice against Blacks in their respective countries. By contrast, he observed that Black Americans "were just socializing, they had turned their back on the cause over here, they were partying."[36] Again, Malcolm X blamed Black Americans for their socioeconomic stagnancy in America by describing their failure to mobilize as a group.

Malcolm X discussed the power of organized Blacks to address the violation of Black human rights internationally. He stated, "This 100 million [individual Blacks] on the inside of the power structure today is what is causing a great deal of concern for the power structure itself."[37] His call to address Black human rights violations aligns with CRT's charge to confront real racial inequalities, rather than to simply theorize about them, and to put White America on notice that oppression, discrimination, and inequality are neither universal nor acceptable. He used these observations to motivate Blacks in the United States to organize, defend themselves, and exercise their civil rights. Specifically, he rebuked Black men for not coming to the defense of a Black woman being brutalized in Selma, Alabama. Malcolm X told Blacks that the government would not do anything to protect Black rights—that such protection was the duty of Blacks themselves, and that it could be accomplished through collective action. Therefore, Malcolm X's call for self-help aimed to empower Blacks as a group, not as individuals. He elucidated: "No, since the federal government has shown that it isn't going to do anything about it but talk, it is a duty, it's your and my duty as men, as human beings, it is our duty to our people, to organize ourselves and let the government know that if they don't stop that Klan, we'll stop it ourselves."[38]

Here again, Malcolm X's reference to self-help is for the benefit of the group as opposed to individual empowerment. Malcolm X continued in his address to say that class does not trump race: "It does not matter if you are an upper-class Negro. Actually, there's no such thing as an upper-class Negro, because he catches the same hell as the other class Negro. All of them catch the same hell, which is one of the things that's good about this racist system—it makes us all one."[39]

In these two passages, Malcolm X's use of the plural first

person "we," his deliberate reference to "our people," and his emphasis on unified suffering make it clear that he spoke with the collective in mind. The discourse of Malcolm X was, in total, a call to Blacks to set aside their differences, embrace the ideology of common fate, and work together for the betterment of all Blacks. However, we can see in his admonishments the beginnings of a more laissez-faire approach to racial inequality; Malcolm X's decision to blame Blacks as a group may have set the stage for a shifting of blame to individual Blacks.

STOKELY CARMICHAEL: COLLECTIVE LEGITIMIZATION OF BLACK INTERESTS

Stokely Carmichael echoed King's and Malcolm X's narratives of collective action and common fate. For example, in his address, "Black Power," at the University of California at Berkeley in October 1966, Carmichael responded to Blacks' lack of power by calling on Blacks to "legitimate" their own actions. In other words, he called on Blacks themselves to deem anything Blacks said or did as legal, regardless of the dominant legal paradigms.[40] Carmichael's view of Black legitimacy speaks to the absence of abstract liberalism in his political outlook. Despite the passage of the Civil Rights Act, Carmichael saw that Blacks were not free, nor did they have equal rights and opportunities.

Carmichael emphasized that Blacks were bound by the color of their skin: "The reason for a man being picked as a slave was . . . because of the color of his skin."[41] This one constant in a sea of variables, Carmichael asserted, was the sole reason that Blacks remained oppressed: "We are oppressed as a group because we are black, not because we are lazy, not because we're apathetic, not because we're stupid, not because we smell, not because we eat watermelon and have good rhythm. We are oppressed because we are black."[42]

Here, Carmichael reminds us of the intellectual history of

racism that began as early as the seventeenth century and continued through Linnaeus, Kant, and Hegel, wherein Blacks have
consistently been denigrated and placed in an inferior position
in the racial hierarchy. He confronts real discrimination against
Blacks and highlights the social power dynamics that keep
Blacks subordinated; in this way, he foreshadows CRT and racial
realism. Carmichael's solution to oppression was to "wield the
group power that one has, not the individual power which this
country then sets the criteria under which a man may come into
it."[43] In other words, collective action, not individual action, was
the key to collective liberation; moreover, the individualistic
emphasis of abstract liberalism can only promote group welfare
if the power structure legitimizes it.

Integration (interest convergence) was, for Carmichael, oppressive for this same reason: it only functions if Whites permit it.
Essentially, Black-White integrationist movements like the civil
rights movement are not meant to serve or advance the political
or socioeconomic interests of Blacks; rather, they are meant to
maintain White dominance and advance White self-interest by
appearing to serve and advance Black socioeconomic progress
and prospects. Other movements that followed this pattern
include the emancipation of American slaves, which preserved
the Union, and the outlawing of Jim Crow discrimination,
which preserved America's dignity on the world stage.

Carmichael flatly rejected the bootstrap philosophy, calling it
"downright lies."[44] He critiqued the egalitarian claim of abstract
liberalism in the following statement: "This country told us that
if we worked hard we would succeed, and if that were true we
would own this country lock, stock, and barrel. . . . It is we who
have picked the cotton for nothing. It is we who are the maids
in the kitchens. . . . It is we who are the janitors, the porters,
the elevator men; we who sweep. . . ."[45] Carmichael concluded
Blacks are the hardest workers and the lowest paid. Contrary
to the abstract liberal idea that those who work hard receive
rewards, Black people, according to Carmichael, have received

little reward for their labor; they are uncompensated even after centuries of slavery.

Critical race theory echoes the call for common fate and collective action that we have seen in the speeches of King, Malcolm X, and Carmichael, all of whom provide evidence against the frames of color-blind racism. Proponents of CRT recognize that racism is widespread and institutional, and that it works as a constraint that keeps Blacks subordinate to and disparate from Whites. In analyzing the above narratives, I have critically explored patterns in and across the discourses and identified the social consequences of these discursive representations of reality. During the civil rights and Black Power eras, these elite discourses helped Blacks to perceive their linked fate, favor collective action, work hard, and take personal responsibility for their collective socioeconomic progress in the face of racial discrimination and policies that failed to address the issue.

JOHN MCWHORTER: BLACK SELF-SABOTAGE THROUGH RACIAL IDENTITY

McWhorter believes that the battle of race is in fact already won, and Blacks need to stop fighting an old war. Black common fate and collective action take center stage, though not favorably, in McWhorter's narratives regarding Black socioeconomic opportunities and outcomes.

Losing the Race

McWhorter, in *Losing the Race: Self-Sabotage in Black America*, blamed Blacks for their marginalization, citing cults of victimology, separatism, and anti-intellectualism. He located Blacks' socioeconomic inequality in collective Black behavior of self-sabotage, rather than in structural racism. "Defeatist thought patterns," he stated, referring to the three cults, make up "the bedrock of black identity."[46] Although McWhorter acknowledged that common fate and collective action, which he disparages, may have at one time been proper in light of overt racial discrimination, he argued that to "dwell upon victimhood [now] rather than work against it would be defeatist, polluting spirits needed for concrete uplift."[47] In other words, it was right for Blacks to band together in the past, but now it is unnecessary and counterproductive. McWhorter said that the continued embrace of the cults of victimology, separatism, and anti-intellectualism in a far less racist society is "a continuous, self-sustaining act of self-sabotage" that allows Blacks to accept cultural racism as the norm and hinders continued Black progress.[48]

How did McWhorter respond to other scholars, such as Dawson, who maintained that airing grievances permits racial injustices to be addressed in politics? In satirical fashion, McWhorter called these grievances the seven "Articles of Faith" of victimology, including the beliefs that most Blacks are poor and three out of four live in the ghetto; that Blacks earn less than Whites for the same job; that racist arson against Black churches is rampant; that the U.S. government funneled crack into South Central Los Angeles; that racism is responsible for the high rates of Black male incarceration; and that police brutality reflects an unchanging racism. While McWhorter demonstrated a classic example of minimization in supporting six of his articles of faith, the seventh, police brutality he stated "does demonstrate racism."[49]

Victimology's articles of faith, McWhorter contended, distort Blacks' factual perception regarding their socioeconomic progress and prospects. These articles of faith encourage Blacks to fixate on and exaggerate vestiges of racism while minimizing positive socioeconomic developments. Thus, McWhorter advocated for Blacks to abandon notions of common fate and collective action, as they are a waste of time. McWhorter argued that, instead of helping, the mindset of eternal victimhood prevents Black socioeconomic parity because it enslaves Blacks, rather than freeing them to individually pursue opportunities.

McWhorter identified what he saw as another flaw in the ideologies of common fate and collection action: separatism. A "natural outgrowth of victimism," separatism persuades Blacks to see themselves as an "unofficial sovereign entity" within an "eternally hostile" White society.[50] The "Cult of Separatism" frames mainstream culture as contemptuous and rejects it as White culture. McWhorter called this a self-destructive response that only serves to disaffect Blacks from White books and education, and from "some of the most well-wrought, emotionally stirring art and ideas that humans have produced."[51] Separatism serves to mire the race "in a parochialism that clips its spiritual wings."[52] Furthermore, separatism denies that the Black situation is improving. Here McWhorter strongly demonstrated his alliance with the post-racial paradigm. More disastrously, according to McWhorter, separatism encourages Blacks to consider themselves as somehow free from "general standards of evaluation."[53] In education, he stated, Blacks demand lower admission standards and all kinds of "special" exemptions and set-asides as a sort of inheritance. But lower standards, McWhorter pointed out, sabotage Black youth by seducing them to lower their own expectations and efforts.

The third maladaptive behavior McWhorter identifies as "a defining feature of cultural blackness today" is anti-intellectualism.[54] McWhorter found anti-intellectualism at "all levels of the black community."[55] He likened anti-intellectualism to a virus that is a residue of the past, when Blacks were banned by Whites from all forms of education. Separatism has exacerbated anti-intellectualism by scorning White culture and framing schooling and books as "suspicious and alien, not to be embraced by the authentically 'black' person."[56] Anti-intellectualism, McWhorter said, is an insidious cultural trait of the Black community, impoverishing Blacks intellectually and spiritually, and preventing them from forging solutions for themselves that may lead to a better future. It is, for McWhorter, Black anti-intellectualism, not structural racism in the form of school underfunding, bigoted teachers, tracking, "black intelligence," stereotype threat, or biased exams, that best explains why Blacks underperform Asians and Whites on average in all subjects, at all educational levels, at all income levels, and by all measures (test scores, grades, and class ranking).[57] Blacks are not barred from academic achievement; they are "leery of it."[58]

Winning the Race

McWhorter continued his indictment of Black common fate and collective action in *Winning the Race: Beyond the Crisis in Black America*.[59] At the core of this narrative was McWhorter's alternate explanation for Black America's continuing problems: the therapeutic-alienation meme. *Therapeutic alienation* is "alienation unconnected to, or vastly disproportionate to, real-life stimulus, but maintained because it reinforces one's sense of psychological legitimacy, via defining oneself against an oppressor characterized as eternally depraved."[60] In other words, a Black person chooses to view himself or herself as oppressed because doing so strengthens his or her personal identity. Elsewhere, McWhorter described this type of alienation as a meme consisting of "thought patterns that become entrenched in society via self-replication from mind to mind."[61] It could then be said that therapeutic alienation inflicted by Whites on Blacks is unconnected to, or vastly disproportionate to, real-life stimulus, but is maintained because it reinforces the White sense of psychological legitimacy. McWhorter characterized therapeutic alienation as a misguided strategy for advancement and self-definition. Referencing Eric Hoffer, McWhorter says that therapeutic alienation is why "individuals . . . so often subsume themselves into ideological movements"[62]; this "very individuality," says Hoffer, "is an unnatural condition . . . so much so that it is almost intolerably threatening to many people."[63] Social movements, said McWhorter, have served their purpose in reducing discrimination; now, he says, it is time for Blacks to "[roll] their sleeves up and [work] out concrete plans for change."[64]

McWhorter explained that therapeutic alienation originated in the counterculture. Invented by Whites, the counterculture encouraged everyone to express their alienation publicly and loudly. The counterculture itself is a form of interest convergence, and it may have promoted the collective action that passed the Voting Rights Act of 1964. But most Whites simply walked away from the concept of alienation when it no longer served their purposes. For Blacks, McWhorter claimed, the alienation stuck; Blacks "took the ball and ran with it."[65] This was devastating in certain parts of the Black community, particularly on Blacks' sense of honor and shame, their sense of responsibility, and the value they placed on effort and persistence. The counterculture, according to McWhorter, inspired the National Welfare Rights Organization to demand access to welfare for all poor Black people, not as a stopgap measure, but as an inalienable, open-ended right, which led to welfare dependency. The counterculture even distorted the views of social thinkers, Black and White alike, such as Piven, Cloward, and Carmichael, who McWhorter claimed crippled Black behavior through denying, making excuses for, and even rationalizing Black misbehavior.[66]

From the late 1960s up to the writing of *Winning the Race: Beyond the Crisis in Black America* in 2005, McWhorter said, racism has radically declined. As a result, Blacks were welcomed as full and equal participants in mainstream American society. But the meme of therapeutic alienation, McWhorter alleged, creates an oppositional behavioral identity, which stagnates Black progress. Rather than striving to be successful as individuals in an equal society, Blacks chose to adopt a meme that permitted them to engage in self-destructive behavior.

McWhorter proposed three solutions to Black self-sabotaging behavior that might rekindle Black socioeconomic progress and prospects.[67] The first solution is a change of consciousness. Rather than fixating on the racism of old, Blacks ought to process the obstacles they face in ways that are appropriate to the new post-racial world. McWhorter claimed that Blacks' current lens, the color-blind frame of naturalization, tells Blacks it is normal for them to be underprivileged and for Whites to be socioeconomically privileged. However, these norms speak to the present, not the past. McWhorter's second solution, rigorous education, suggests that as long as Black students are not expected to adhere to rigorous academic standards, they will continue to have substandard academic performance. Blacks' poor school performance, according to McWhorter, is the result of behavioral factors such as the therapeutic-alienation meme. Although the narrative perpetuated in both word and deed about Black academic expectations is not one that originated with Blacks, the solution to it rests in the hands of Black students and their educators. The final solution proposed by McWhorter, new Black leadership, suggests that new Black leaders are desperately needed. New Black leaders will be more concerned with the future than the past, will not only highlight Black failures but celebrate Black victories and success, and will not focus on racism and discrimination as the reason for Black stagnated progress.

Discussion and Evidence to the Contrary

McWhorter's narrative of post-racial Black stagnation has much to recommend to a Black public with an interest in moving forward rather than dwelling in the past. Indeed, as Ron Eyerman suggested, Black collective identity may be viewed as a cultural defense against the collective trauma of slavery in the United States.[68] As with trauma at the individual level, collective trauma may be characterized by the formation of defensive structures (in this case, Black collectivism), which although important for survival in the face of the traumatic event itself, may become obstacles to normal functioning when they are carried forward into nontraumatic situations. In order to fully recover from the trauma, such defensive structures must ultimately be recognized as no longer necessary and dismantled. Thus, McWhorter's view can be taken to represent a natural, healing impulse, by which the Black community desires to free itself from a collective identity, Black identity, that is inextricably linked to a traumatic past. By eschewing the notion of Black collective identity, and hence Black linked fate, McWhorter attempted to liberate individual Blacks, enabling them to define themselves with respect to a nontraumatic present.

However compelling it is, this attitude is founded on the assumption that the present is indeed nontraumatic—a view that may itself be overly ebullient, given the social and economic facts of contemporary life. Sociologist William Mangino and economist Patrick L. Mason offered empirical evidence that contradicts McWhorter's claims. They found that, after controlling for socioeconomic status, Blacks actually have greater educational attainment than Whites.[69] Furthermore, it is far from clear that Blacks ever demanded lower standards and special exemptions. Indeed, evidence from the civil rights era, including *Brown v. Board of Education,* suggested that they have demanded constitutional and civil rights precisely equal to those enjoyed by Whites. Such evidence suggests that the trauma of inequality and institutionalized racism, although less overt and violent today than in the days of slavery, is still very much ongoing.

Black socioeconomic statistics also provide evidence to refute McWhorter's claims of self-destructive behavior and point to structural explanations, including policy shifts away from affirmative action. For example, John Bound and Richard B. Freeman pointed out that racial behavioral factors from the mid-1970s through the 1980s were not, in contradiction to McWhorter's suggestion, sufficient to explain the stagnation and erosion of Black socioeconomic parity.

The increased differentiation of the Black population post-1964, evinced in the development of an elite of college graduates and professionals on the one side and of labor force dropouts and criminal offenders on the other, makes any unicausal explanation difficult to sustain. This does not mean, however, that the erosion is inexplicable. To the contrary, much of the change is attributed to quantifiable but different shifts in the relative demand and supply of specific groups that occurred against the backdrop of weakened affirmative action and equal opportunity pressures. The economic decline of inner cities, loss of manufacturing jobs, fall in the real minimum wage, and drop in union density underlie, for example, the erosion of relative earnings among men with high school or less education, particularly. Growth of crime went hand-in-hand with the joblessness of high school dropouts. Occupational downgrading, possibly due to weakened affirmative action and shifts in demand toward the most highly skilled, and a huge increase in the ratio of black-to-white college graduates reduced the relative earnings of black college graduates.[70]

William Darity and Darrick Hamilton reported that in 2008, the median hourly wage for Black male full-time workers was $14.90, while the median for White male counterparts was nearly $6 higher, at $20.84.[71] This disparity was not due primarily to differences in educational attainment, because disparities persist within educational categories: Black males with a high school degree or a bachelor's degree earned only 74% of what White males in the same educational category earned; among high school dropouts, Black males earned a mere 61% of what their White male counterparts earned.[72] Further, nearly 90 percent of U.S. professions can be considered racially segregated, even after factoring in differences of educational attainment. That is, Black males are more likely to hold low-wage jobs.

Neither is there much evidence to support McWhorter's claim that Blacks undervalue educational performance. After scouring existing research, Karolyn Tyson, William Darity, and Domini R. Castellino found little to no evidence to support the thesis that high-performing Black students are accused of acting White (the "acting White thesis"). Moreover, they found only two studies that quantitatively examined the acting White thesis at the time of their study, and in both cases, the thesis was not confirmed.[73] Instead, the researchers' interviews with Black middle and high school students in North Carolina revealed "an expressed desire to do well academically."[74] The one school out of the forty they examined where the burden of acting White regarding academic achievement was observed had a segregated curriculum. Although it was a racially mixed school, the researchers observed a highly segregated advanced-placement curriculum where few Blacks were enrolled in advanced courses. The authors found the perception, among both Blacks and Whites in the school, that academic success was the domain of White students.

ANDRA GILLESPIE: GAPS IN BLACK LEADERSHIP

Whose Black Politics?

In her 2010 book *Whose Black Politics?: Cases in Post-Racial Black Leadership,* Andra Gillespie presented a framework for understanding young, Black, and post-racial (in Gillespie's terms, "Phase III") leaders and their tendency to be racially moderate and less race-oriented while simultaneously espousing Black political rhetoric. Citing James Traub, Gillespie defined Phase III leaders as those born after 1960 or immediately before or after the passage of all the major civil rights legislation. Factors that frame the political identities of Phase III Black leaders include crossover appeal, perceived career trajectory, and connections to the Black establishment. Crossover appeal, whereby Black candidates strive to appeal to the White electorate, forces candidates to develop policy agendas that are less militant and more moderate on the militant–moderate scale. Among the Black electorate, as a result, there is no focus on Blacks' collective policy interests, since crossover appeal also diverts Black attention. Perceived career trajectory speaks to credible aspirations, in the eyes of the electorate, for state or national office. Those with long career trajectories tend to be "young, well educated, and less committed to purely partisan politics."[75] Connections

to the Black establishment influence candidates' political social-
ization, either through birth or work relationships, implying a
degree of linked fate with the political status quo, and not with
the Black population as a whole.

Do these Phase III Black leaders link their political success to
the Black community, or are they individualists ascending the
political ranks on their own merits? Gillespie stated, "Implicit in
this discussion of new Black politicians is their relative chance
for success and the means by which they emerge onto the political spectrum."[76] Citing Martin, Gillespie referenced Ronald
Walters's interview in *Savoy* magazine, where Walters demonstrated lack of trust in Phase III Black leaders as "merely a tool
of White elites who wanted to replace more acerbic, older Black
leaders with less threatening, younger Black leaders."[77] Walters
declared: "[The White power structure] would rather supplant
[the old guard] with a far more accommodating leadership.
They are going to pit them against the so-called old leadership
because they have been threatened by the interests and power
of the Black leadership who really have the influence and control of Black people."[78]

Abstract liberalism, as Bonilla-Silva defined it, is the most
important frame of color blindness, stating that there is no systemic racism and that every individual is equal and free. Under
that assumption, it would no longer be necessary for Blacks to
associate with a Black establishment to ascend to political office.
Therefore, color blindness would be in evidence much more
than it is today if Phase III Black leaders actually ascended the
political (or organizational) ladder on their own individual
merits.

True to the long-standing dynamism of Black politics, Gilles-
pie identified eight types of Phase III Black leaders: (1) Ivy
League Upstarts; (2) Local Kids Made Good; (3) Rebrands of
Their Parents; (4) Deracialized Sequels; (5) Chips Off the Old
Block; (6) New "Old Standard Bearers"; (7) New Activists; and
(8) Rebels Without a Chance. This politically and stylistically

diverse new Black leadership has reignited concern about "the efficacy of racial moderation."[79] In other words, racially moderate Phase III leaders may not be able to "address explicitly racial issues" because "deracialized political candidates made a Faustian bargain with . . . non-Black constituents to not address racial issues in exchange for getting elected."[80] By conforming to the frames of color blindness, Gillespie argued, Phase III Black leaders lose the ability to promote Black interests.

Of the eight types of Phase III Black Leaders, only four have strong ties to the Black establishment. These include Rebrands (e.g., Harold Ford), Deracialized Sequels (e.g., Keiffer Mitchell), Chips Off the Old Block (e.g., Yvette Clarke and Kwame Kilpatrick), and New "Old Standard Bearers" (e.g., Jesse Jackson Jr. and Kendrick Meek). Of these four, only two, Rebrands and New "Old Standard Bearers," have a realistically perceived trajectory for higher elected office. While Rebrands are said to have high crossover appeal, their relationship with Black establishments and racially radical parents could frighten White voters. Similarly, New "Old Standard Bearers" would not be successful because they do not appeal to White voters. If Gillespie has characterized Phase III Black leaders correctly, Black politics seems to have little chance of reaching the mainstream.

The shift to states' rights under Reagan ushered in rollbacks of policies that had created socioeconomic advantages for Blacks. This "Reagan Revolution" was accomplished through bureaucratic control. Reagan's appointments to the Equal Employment Opportunity Commission (EEOC), the Office of Federal Contract Compliance Programs (OFCCP), and federal courts, including the United States Supreme Court, subscribed to anti–affirmative action ideologies.[81] Resulting budget and staff reductions enabled Reagan to undermine the socioeconomic effectiveness of race-conscious affirmative action without reversing it. The net effect was a reversal of the policies that had led to gains, which left Blacks vulnerable to stagnated and widening socioeconomic gaps. This is a case in point for the importance of gaining federal office to racial equality, and it shows why any hope of addressing Black socioeconomic parity at the policy level could only come with Rebrands or New "Old Standard Bearers," since they have longer career trajectories and could make it to the federal level. Deracialized Sequels with high crossover appeal often choose not to run for higher office, and Chips Off the Old Block do not appeal to White voters, in part because they respond to pressure to "maintain the political status quo, even if it hurts Black advancement," but only unwillingly.[82] Thus, White voters view them as insufficiently deracialized. Furthermore, even if Rebrands and New "Old Standard Bearers" make it to federal political positions, any shift to states' rights could still rebuff the implementation of race-conscious federal policies. As such, race-conscious policies do not appear to be the right way to address Black socioeconomic stagnation.

Phase III leadership types with weak connections to Black establishments include Ivy League Upstarts (e.g., Cory Booker, Artur Davis, and Barack Obama), Local Kids Made Good (e.g., Anthony Brown, Adrien Fenty, Kevin Johnson, Heather McTeer-Hudson, and Laura Richardson), New Activists (e.g., Keith Ellison), and Rebels Without a Chance (e.g., Markel Hutchins and Kevin Powell). Ivy League Upstarts like former president Obama, former congressman Artur Davis, and senator Cory Booker have high crossover appeal, but Black communities criticize these leaders on the grounds that they use Blacks for their personal political gain.[83] Like the Ivy League Upstarts, Local Kids Made Good have high crossover appeal and have weak ties to Black communities, but they choose not to pursue higher elected office. New Activists, by contrast, are racialized and controversial, lacking the crossover appeal they would need for political success. They seem to come along in times of exacerbated class division among upper- and lower-class Blacks, and they may be elected at local levels thanks to cohesive voting blocs of lower-class Blacks and to populist appeal to poor non-Blacks. Rebels Without a Chance are characterized by being disconnected from

Black establishments as well as White voters, and they only gain political traction when there is large-scale grassroots support from "disaffected Black voters who would almost certainly have to comprise a majority of the electorate."[84] Of the four types with weak connections to Black establishments, only the Ivy League Upstarts and New Activists have a perceived trajectory for higher elected national office.[85]

Gillespie concluded that Phase III Black leaders are neither powerful nor senior enough in the aggregate to impact the Black agenda as it relates to legislation that advances the socioeconomic interests of Blacks. She suggested that "we will eventually have to ask whether the campaign, legislative, and governing approach of this new generation of politicians will actually be more successful in delivering goods and services to African-American communities."[86] Furthermore, Gillespie cites Robert Smith's prediction that deracialization will not only fail to help Blacks socioeconomically, but will also reorient Black leadership away from issues of Black socioeconomic parity. In other words, since Phase III Black leaders overwhelmingly reject the structural reality of racism, their policies will not target Black socioeconomic stagnation directly enough to produce necessary change. If Smith is correct, Blacks can look forward to intensified marginalization that may lead to even more strongly divided Black communities.

Gillespie astutely noted that Blacks' fixation on White happiness with Black candidates, as opposed to Black candidates who are best able to represent interests of Blacks, is anathema to Black policy interests. The political views of Phase III Black leaders, such as increasing economic opportunity for individuals of color and school vouchers, agree with the political attitudes of the Black electorate of the same generation.[87] The paradox, then, is that Blacks engage in self-destructive behaviors in their promotion of certain candidates. Specifically, Blacks subvert their own policy interests when they fixate on White approval ratings of Black candidates instead of those Black candidates' ability to represent Black interests.

Viewing these aims through a lens informed by critical race theory suggests that Whites will vote for a deracialized candidate who shares their policy preferences; after all, Black candidates can rarely get elected to state or national office without the overwhelming support of White voters. In this way, most post-racial Black leaders and the Black electorate align with a color-blind ethos and likely do not see the need for race-conscious policies. The civil rights movement, in their view, has provided ample opportunity for equality, and there is no longer a need to focus explicitly on race issues.

Although institutional barriers constrained post–civil rights ("Phase I") Black leadership (like mayor Carl Stokes of Cleveland, mayor Richard G. Hatcher of Gary, Indiana, representative Shirley Chisholm of New York, representative John Lewis of Georgia, and senator Edward Brooke of Massachusetts), its focus on collective action resulted in a movement toward Black economic parity.[88] Such a call to action is largely absent today under Phase III Black leadership. The power of collective action may, therefore, be muted.

Gillespie on Ebullience

Andra Gillespie offered an explanation for why Barack Obama's ebullience resonated so strongly with Americans after the 2008 election. She stated that America was still in the afterglow of President Obama's election, and that Blacks also found themselves affected by this aura.[89] The afterglow theory was corroborated by the Pew Charitable Trust's 2010 Study *A Year After Obama's Election Blacks Upbeat About Progress, Prospects*, which inspired the present analysis.

Although there is no monolithic Black political agenda or standard in Black politics, I contend that, because Black candidates generally need overwhelming White support to win elections, the standard of electability will be individualism, which means "deemphasizing racial issues, presenting a nonthreaten-

ing demeanor and limiting race-specific appeals to Black constituents."[90] In the light of Gillespie's reference to the anathema that
is Blacks' focus on candidates that appeal to Whites, Black ebullience is more symbolic than substantive. Policy interests relative
to Black socioeconomic parity do not serve the interests of the
dominant power structure, as evidenced by Obama's behavioral
solutions to structural racism. Given the systemic changes produced by the openly racial discourses of Phase I Black leaders
(the first wave of elected Black officials in the post–civil rights era
in the 1970s), having a Black president who failed to articulate
structural impediments related to stagnated Black socioeconomic
parity, refused to advocate for universally targeted policies to
address stagnation, and would only call for individual responsibility was an anathema to Blacks as well.

BARACK OBAMA: COMMON FATE
AND COLLECTIVE ACTION

Barack Obama takes the spotlight in our analysis of paradoxical
ebullience because his presidency coincided with the uplift in
Black optimism that characterizes this paradox. When Obama
was a senator and running for the presidency, linked fate and
collective action appeared as overt themes in his narratives;
however, these ideas appear in more nuanced forms in his
presidential discourses. I explore Obama's 2013 commencement address to Morehouse College, a liberal arts and a historically black college (HBCU) that graduates predominately
Black males, and his 2012 commencement address to Barnard
College, a liberal arts college that graduates predominately
White females. I have chosen to compare these commencement
speeches to determine if Obama made similar demands and
offered similar advice in the areas of personal responsibility
and socioeconomic parity depending on the audience.

Commencement Address to Morehouse College

In his commencement speech at Morehouse College to the class of 2013, President Obama told the graduating class of their collective responsibilities: "There are some things as Morehouse Men . . . you are obliged to do for those still left behind."[91] The underprivileged to whom President Obama referred, include those living "in troubled neighborhoods . . . many of them heavily African American."[92] He also referred to those impacted by the structural impediments of scarce jobs and wages, underfunded schools, and pervasive violence; these underprivileged "spend their youth not behind a desk in a classroom, but hanging out on the streets brooding behind a jail cell."[93] In this passage, Obama seemed to portray young men of color as incidental victims of cultural racism; at the same time, he recognized that there are structural impediments that take Black men out of educative settings and put them behind bars. President Obama recounted his own experiences with collective responsibility and the "sense of connection and empathy—the special obligation I felt as a Black man . . . to help those who need it most."[94] And President Obama invoked Black history to inspire collective action when he said, "You now hail from a lineage and legacy of immeasurably strong men—who bore tremendous burdens and still laid the stones for the path on which we now walk. You wear the mantle of Frederick Douglass and Booker T. Washington, and Ralph Bunche and Langston Hughes, and George Washington Carver and Ralph Abernathy and Thurgood Marshall, and yes, Dr. Martin Luther King, Jr."[95]

In all of these excerpts, President Obama's reminder to the Morehouse graduates is tinged with linked fate and collective responsibility. He stated an expectation that the individual example of the Morehouse graduates' hard work, personal responsibility, and "special insight" resulting from "the sting of discrimination" would catalyze a movement to improve the socioeconomic position of Black men; after all, Obama said, Morehouse graduates know what it means to "overcome barriers."[96] In hindsight, the movement Obama was likely referencing was his My Brother's Keeper initiative, launched in February 2014. These individual examples, according to Fredrick Harris in *The Price of the Ticket: Barack Obama and Rise and Decline of Black Politics*, can translate into the uplift, echoing W. E. B. Du Bois's notion of the "Talented Tenth," whose role it was to be a moral compass, and standard bearer of sorts, to the remaining nine-tenths of Blacks.[97]

While emphasizing collective action and common fate, President Obama also blamed Black individuals for their own suffering. He stated, "Too many young men in [our] community continue to make bad choices" and then to make excuses for those choices.[98] While Obama acknowledged that "the bitter legacy of slavery and segregation" still impacts life chances, he also stressed that the Morehouse class of 2013 had "no time for excuses," and that, despite the apparent effects of structural racism, Blacks must not blame structural racism for their lower socioeconomic parity with "millions of young people from China and India and Brazil . . . many of whom started with a whole lot less than [the Morehouse class of 2013] did."[99] Two paradoxes are evident in these passages: one, the simultaneous blaming and pardoning of structural racism for Black suffering; and two, a superficial addressing of structural problems by means of moral uplift.

While still ambiguous in the above passages, Obama's stance became decidedly color-blind in the passages that follow. For instance, President Obama made it clear to Morehouse graduates in 2013 that their struggles were insignificant: "Nobody cares how tough your upbringing was. Nobody cares if you suffered some discrimination. And moreover, you have to remember that whatever you've gone through, it pales in comparison to the hardships previous generations endured—and they overcame them. And if they overcame them, you can overcome them too."[100]

This passage in particular reveals Obama's allegiance to minimization, the frame of color-blind racism that holds that racism no longer exists to a large enough degree to impede Blacks socio-economically. Despite acknowledging the role racism plays in Blacks' life chances, President Obama told this group that, no matter what, they cannot point to racism as the reason that they do not have socioeconomic parity. Moreover, Obama invoked a host of successful Blacks who pioneered the struggle for Black interests and charged the Morehouse class of 2013 to follow their example: "These men were many things to many people. And they knew full well the role that racism played in their lives. But when it came to their own accomplishments and sense of purpose, they had no time for excuses."[101] Obama implied that the Black heroes he mentioned did not complain about structural racism; instead, they simply took action as individuals. He made this claim despite the fact that certain Black heroes, such as Martin Luther King Jr., did in fact speak out about structural problems.[102] In short, Obama's words appear empowering but in fact bespeak his allegiance to the color-blind principle of abstract liberalism; he asserted that freedom, individualism, and egalitarianism have provided such opportunities for Blacks that racism can no longer have a significant effect on Black prospects.

President Obama's color blindness appears again and again throughout the speech at Morehouse, including in his proclamation that previous generations endured and overcame their hardships. The reality is that previous generations, based on socioeconomic indicators, particularly wealth, did not overcome them. Yet Obama was ebullient: "And I promise you, what was needed in Dr. Mays's time, that spirit of excellence, and hard work, and dedication, and no excuses is needed now more than ever. . . . But if you stay hungry, if you keep hustling, if you keep on your grind and get other folks to do the same—nobody can stop you."[103] To summarize, at the same time that Obama acknowledged the socioeconomic effects of structural racism, he also discouraged Blacks from blaming structural racism for their socioeconomic problems, and charged Blacks with the task of pulling themselves up by their own bootstraps just as he alleged their Black forefathers did.

Commencement Address to Barnard College

In President Obama's 2012 commencement speech at Barnard, he invoked the concept of linked fate in his advice to "never underestimate the power of your example."[104] He continued as follows:

> The very fact that you are graduating, let alone that more women now graduate from college than men, is only possible because earlier generations of women—your mothers, your grandmothers, your aunts—shattered the myth that you couldn't or shouldn't be where you are. This diploma opens up new possibilities, so reach back, convince a young girl to earn one, too. If you earned your degree in areas where we need more women—like computer science or engineering—reach back and persuade another student to study it too. . . . Be a mentor. Be a role model. Until a girl can imagine herself, can picture herself as a computer programmer, or a combatant commander, she won't become one. Until there are women who tell her . . . focus instead on studying and inventing and competing and leading.[105]

As in his speech at Morehouse, Obama's call for collective action in the Barnard speech was tempered by individualism and personal responsibility to the point that individual action alone is what makes socioeconomic parity possible. As he did at Morehouse, Obama told this group of predominately White females that they would have to be responsible and work hard for what they wanted. These short excerpts make the point clear: "It will be up to you"; "You've got to want it"; "It will not be handed to you"; and, "Now that new doors have been opened for you, you've got an obligation to seize those opportunities."[106]

Unlike his speech at Morehouse, in which Obama told the Black men that nobody cared about what they had to endure, the Barnard speech contained consolation for the women: "It's up to you to hold the system accountable and sometimes upend it entirely. It's up to you to stand up and to be heard, to write and to lobby, to march, to organize, to vote."[107] These were clear calls to collective action and to engage in counter storytelling (one of the key concepts of CRT). Obama told the Barnard Class of 2012 to let the world know of the injustices committed against (White) women. For White women, it is time to "upend" the system; for Black men, it is time to stop making excuses.

Address to the 99th Annual Convention of the NAACP

In his 2008 address to the 99th Annual Convention of the NAACP, then-senator Obama emphasized common fate.[108] He pointed to the collective action of generations past and its role in the socioeconomic gains experienced by Blacks in general and the elevation of Obama himself as the Democratic nominee. "It is a powerful reminder," he says, "of the debt we all owe to those who marched for us and fought for us."[109] At the same time, Obama's speech revealed that he values individual responsibility to promote the common good; he remembered "all those whose names never made it into the history books . . . who had the courage to remake the world as it should be."[110] He told those gathered that if he were elected president, he would continue to fight to correct the "barriers of prejudice as earlier generations stood up for him."[111] In this narrative, Obama called for collective action as a way to gain socioeconomic parity for Blacks. Referencing Martin Luther King Jr. and Roy Wilkins, Obama claimed that "social justice is not enough," and stated that he has "been working his entire adult life to build an America where social justice is being served and economic justice is being served, an America where we all have an equal chance to make it if we try."[112] In the manner of King, he reminded those gathered that, "our work is not over."[113] This "work" included improvements to education, corporate accountability, elimination of poverty, and growing the middle class; in addition, "it's about the responsibilities we all share for the future we hold in common."[114] Clearly, the audience at the meeting of the NAACP not only had a common fate, but their fate was tied to the effects of racial prejudice, and they were encouraged to act as a collective to overcome those effects.

In this same speech, Obama followed demands for responsibility on Wall Street and Washington with a demand for Black responsibility. "If we're serious about reclaiming that dream, we have to do more in our own lives, our own families, and our own communities."[115] Though this parallel has rhetorical value, its factual value is more questionable; Blacks as a group have not been "personally irresponsible" to the point of capsizing the U.S. economy. In response to remarks such as this, Harris, referencing Cornell Belcher, noted that "Obama became one of the most individualized blacks in this country."[116] The implication here is that changing individual Black behavior will change the social and economic injustice experienced by Blacks.

In these three speeches, a double standard is evident in Obama's treatment of Black people and White women. As is clear from my discussion of Obama's speech to the women of Barnard in 2012, Obama conceded that systemic injustice has in part caused the socioeconomic disparity between White women and men; in fact, he encouraged White women to challenge the system. By contrast, Obama was less willing to allow Black people to blame anyone but themselves for their socioeconomic disparity, and he implored them as individuals to take advantage of their freedoms to make changes in their socioeconomic prospects. Obama inspired similar ideas of linked fate and collective action among White women and Black people, but his charges to Black people tend to be grounded in questionable interpretations of Black history. Altogether, the discrepancies between Obama's treatment of White issues and Black issues, as well as between his treatment of said issues before and after his election, signal the influence of the frames of color blindness on his discursive representation of reality.

Obama on Ebullience

In President Obama's discourses on Black socioeconomic parity, he presents a notion of Black progress as a steady upward trend—a cause for ebullience. In so doing, he appears to subscribe uncritically to the idea of racial progress generally. For instance, in his speech at Morehouse to the class of 2013, President Obama said, "Now, think about it. For black men in the '40s and the '50s, the threat of violence, the constant humiliations, large and small, the uncertainty that you could support a family, the gnawing doubts born of the Jim Crow culture that told you every day that somehow you were inferior, the temptation to shrink from the world, to accept your place, to avoid risks, to be afraid—that temptation was necessarily strong."[117] He continued: "And over the last 50 years, . . . barriers have come tumbling down, and new doors of opportunity have swung open, and laws and hearts and minds have been changed to the point where someone who looks just like you can somehow come to serve as President of these United States of America. So the history we share should give you hope. The future we share should give you hope. You're graduating into an improving job market.[118] You're living in a time when advances in technology and communication put the world at your fingertips."[119]

In these passages, Obama aimed to create ebullience in his audience using the frames of color-blind racism. Things are not as bad as they once were, he said (minimization). The opportunities are there for the taking, he said (abstract liberalism). If these assertions are true, and Obama implies that they are, then Blacks are failing to prosper simply because they are not trying, not walking through the doors of opportunity. In sum, Blacks have every reason to believe that things will get better for them; they should be ebullient.

Ebullience was also manifest in President Obama's speech to the graduating class of Barnard in 2012. He told these White women that despite "a steady stream of sensationalism and scandal and stories . . . that suggest change isn't possible," they should be optimistic.[120] Obama was "convinced [that they, the women] are tougher."[121] In other words, (White) women should be ebullient on account of their individual ability to counteract systemic difficulties. The question, continued Obama, "is not whether things will get better—they always do."[122] This is optimism in its purest form; it predicts inevitable improvement. In closing, Obama indicates, "Now more than ever . . . if you persevere in what you decide to do with your life, I have every faith not only that you will succeed, but that, through you, our nation will continue to be a beacon of light."[123] It seems from Obama's discourse that, in the light of the allegedly unprecedented systemic bias in White women's favor, White women have no reason *not* to be optimistic about improving their socioeconomic parity.

A similar ebullience radiated from Obama's speech to the NAACP in 2008, in which he stated that those who love America can change it for the better. Today's America, he noted, is the America that the NAACP has been "fighting for over the past 99 years."[124] Interestingly Blacks had been individually and collectively enfranchised de jure for 143 years before Obama's speech in 2008. In theory, Blacks would not have needed continued collective struggle if legislation were the solution to Black equality. This case in point demonstrates that, contrary to what Obama seems to believe, collective action remains vital to Black progress.

Nevertheless, the Black individualism narrative that Obama espoused in the Morehouse address seems to have widespread appeal among the Black public, and we should make a robust attempt to understand the arguments that support it. Such an understanding will allow us to see why Blacks, from a psychosocial perspective, might be especially attracted to the post-racial narrative at this point in history. This is necessary because the post-racial move is more subtle than a simple erasure of socioeconomic realities, whatever negative consequences it might ultimately have for Black Americans. As we saw in chapter 1, post-race and post-Blackness theories provide one perspective, suggesting that Blacks will be better off on an individual level if they embrace these ideologies. Another possible solution can be found in recent interpretations of the work of pragmatist philosopher, John Dewey. For example, Eddie S. Glaude Jr. suggested that, from a pragmatic perspective of achieving Black socioeconomic progress, it might be counterproductive to continue to rely on the discourse of the civil rights era, which might blind us to new and innovative ideas that would move us forward.[125] From this perspective, Black individualism could be a stepping-stone, releasing Blacks from the now-constraining framework of civil rights and enabling them to discover new ideas that will lead the way forward.

In the above critical discourse analyses, I have explored patterns in and across the discourses and identified certain social consequences of these discursive representations of reality. On the whole, post-racial representations of reality call for a retreat from the notions of linked fate and collective action and more emphasis on individual responsibility, while at the same time advocating a collective change in Black attitudes, norms, and behaviors to address their stagnated socioeconomic progress.

SUMMARY

This analysis presents evidence that civil rights– and Black Power–era discourses were strongly related to collective action and, to a much lesser extent, ebullience. Civil rights leaders, in fact, discouraged extreme optimism, viewing it as an impediment to progress. In contrast, the post-racial era has ushered in an increasingly ebullient discourse that minimizes collective action through an abstract liberal perspective of individualism and personal responsibility. These findings are consistent with my hypotheses: on the one hand, purported Black socioeconomic ebullience and individualistic attitudes may diminish

Black collective action to address socioeconomic stagnation; on the other, there is a decline in Black belief in linked fate and collective action, potentially jeopardizing legislation that provides socioeconomic benefits to Blacks. Given the context of those implications, race conscious universal policy solutions may be a way to address these implications. Additionally, reversing the decline of a belief in common fate and such useful tactics as collective action may require a social movement to align Black racial attitudes with Black socioeconomic reality.

Black elites of the civil rights and Black Power eras shaped Black public discourse to align Black racial attitudes with both the reality of Black socioeconomic disparity and the interests of the dominant power structure. As demonstrated by the current public discourse about Black socioeconomic parity, post-racial Black elites exert control over the public narrative in ways that contradict Black socioeconomic realities and support abuses of power. In this regard, Black racial attitudes about socioeconomic stagnation have changed. The inherent complexity and instability of communication, as described by van Dijk, highlights the bounded nature of discursive power.[126] Discursive power can be overcome. Those who are marginalized can resist elite power structures created by words. The power of discourse can be constrained (bounded by context, for example) and resisted. These findings should help Blacks engage in counter storytelling by reframing their understanding of Black socioeconomic attainment with a greater emphasis on both racial and socioeconomic realism.

The history of Black voting, irrespective of socioeconomic status or other cleavages, suggests that it is influenced by a sense of common fate.[127] This trend may be in danger of reversal, given the finding demonstrated here that socioeconomic ebullience and individualistic attitudes diminish Black collective action to address socioeconomic stagnation. By contrast, less optimism seems to mean more effective action. In Greer's analysis of data from 2004 through 2006, she found that ethnically diverse, unionized Blacks who were not optimistic about their socioeconomic position acted collectively through lobbying, protesting, and ultimately supporting political candidates who supported policy positions that provided socioeconomic benefits for Black union members.[128] Ebullience, then, paradoxically entrenches Blacks in the stagnation about which they feel so optimistic.

The findings of this study also support the hypothesis that a decline in collective action among Blacks will jeopardize policies that provide socioeconomic benefits to Blacks. Again, Greer demonstrated, it was only in the context of a fraternal order that Black Americans formed allegiances with immigrant Blacks, when they otherwise would not have done so.[129] This analysis has shown that the problem extends up the political ladder; post-racial Black elites willingly subvert the Black political agenda for personal political gain, by neither expressly addressing structural barriers related to stagnated Black socioeconomic parity nor advocating for universally targeted policies to address stagnation and only calling for individual responsibility.

But the question remains: To what extent do these discursive trends affect the way Blacks perceive themselves and their emancipation? Are social race narratives sufficient to influence the degree to which change is possible? Do post-racial narratives discourage collective action merely in theory, or also in practice? The answers to these questions are crucial, both for establishing an understanding of how narratives of race function in society, and for proactively creating a discursive environment that enables positive social progress. I turn to these questions in the next chapter.

CHAPTER 4

Social Knowledge and Black "Progress"

The preceding analysis has established a clear trend toward post-racial narratives that encourage Blacks to view themselves as individuals rather than as members of a collective. Black identity is viewed as dangerous to progress, as a form of self-sabotage that encourages Blacks to remain impoverished, incarcerated, and economically disadvantaged. This tendency to "dwell upon victimhood," as John McWhorter and the post-racial representatives have it, is supposed by its proponents to be counterproductive to Black progress. In its stead, Blacks are encouraged to follow the example of successful Blacks like Barack Obama, who have catered to the status quo and received the reward of high stature. Indeed, as we saw in the last chapter, Obama himself has, in his public discourse, strongly encouraged young Blacks to adopt individualist, colorblind views in their struggle for success.

Although this trend in discourse is amply established, it remains to be seen to what extent this shift from the collectivist attitude of the 1950s and 1960s to the individualist attitude of our present times has translated to a difference in thought and action writ large. Has the change in rhetoric led to a change in Blacks' views of and efforts toward their emancipation? To be sure, such a change in attitude and action is well supported by empirical data. As we saw at the outset of this investigation, Blacks were more optimistic about their own economic situation during the Obama era than they had been in twenty-five years, with fully 56 percent of Blacks reporting that the standard-of-living gap between Whites and Blacks had narrowed in the preceding decade.[1] What draws us back to this statistic is its surprising contrast with economic fact, which tells us that the gap in Black-White unemployment has scarcely narrowed in forty-five years,[2] and the wealth gap stands at six Black cents to every White dollar.[3] In order to understand and counteract this paradoxical ebullience, we must establish a connection between anticollectivist discourse and irrational Black optimism. As we shall see, this connection is related to the power of discourse to frame the way in which social actors respond to direct action.

DISCOURSE AND ACTION IN THE CIVIL RIGHTS ERA: THE ROLE OF RELIGION

As we begin to work toward this goal, we must first examine the connection between discourse and action in the collectivist era. The connection between civil rights–era rhetoric and the civil rights legislation of the 1960s is almost everywhere taken for granted. In particular, scholars have placed strong emphasis on the role of the Black church in disseminating information, spreading ideas, and providing meeting space for planning collective action. Fredrick Harris's *Something Within* is the classic text on this topic. Harris demonstrated the complexity of the religious experience in Black communities, arguing that it promotes collective action along both organizational and psychological lines. By providing resources like communication networks, social interaction, and meeting space, churches have enabled political discussion in Black communities. Further, by motivating members to become engaged in moral issues, by spreading information about political candidates and issues, and by developing group consciousness, churches have historically contributed to both voting patterns and more involved forms of collective action.[4]

Harris's study is particularly interesting for its use of quantitative analysis to support the hypothesis of religion as a political resource. He examined the correlation between religious activity and political commitment among Blacks and found a positive correlation between church attendance and voting frequency. Moreover, Harris's results showed that Blacks who feel more strongly religious (i.e., who have a stronger sense of their connection to a god) are more likely to be involved in politics and possess a greater degree of political knowledge. These factors, in turn, translated directly to increased political action.[5]

This connection is, however, not without its critics, among whom Martin Luther King Jr. and Malcolm X are prominent. Both King and Malcolm X criticized Christian religious institutions for their apathy and refusal to engage in earthly matters like politics.[6] Harris argues that the potentially neutralizing effect of religious discourse entered into tension, in the civil rights era, with the church's status as a political resource. The result was, on the one hand, an increased motivation for collective action and, on the other, a channeling of the acceptable forms such action could take. Instead of directly and violently opposing the status quo, the civil rights movement achieved success through nonviolence, voter mobilization, and interest convergence (as we saw in chapter 2). King, who was a minister himself, spearheaded these strategies, thereby bringing a degree of Christian legitimacy to the movement. It was, therefore, through this convergence of political and religious discourse that the concrete strategies of collective action took shape and attained their greatest successes. When, in the later 1960s, the phase of nonviolent direct action began to taper off and gave way to Black Power and more violent, less officially sanctioned forms of collective action, religion again provided a discursive connection in the form of a resurgence of Islamic nationalism, with Malcolm X himself being a leader of the Nation of Islam movement.[7]

BEYOND CIVIL RIGHTS AND BEYOND RELIGION

The importance of religious communities in disseminating information and discourse and thus promoting collective action has also been documented in the post-racial era. But as Blacks have achieved a greater degree of nominal opportunity, churches have been viewed less and less as venues for fomenting change. This phenomenon is compounded by a sense that religious life is a stronghold of self-determination in the Black community, immune from control by the White majority and by status-quo interests. As Kareem Crayton concisely puts it, "The church remains the lone point of contact in black public life that has remained largely protected from regulation by the larger society. [Political] dissent rarely finds a home in the religious discourse of churches because it is regarded as a challenge to the minister or perhaps a substantive rejection of doctrine and teaching."[8] This dynamic echoes the pre–civil rights era, when, as W. E. B. Du Bois described, Blacks were paradoxically brought into agreement with dominant White discourse, which viewed Black prejudice as "the natural defense of culture against barbarism, learning against ignorance, purity against crime."[9] When framed in these terms, Du Bois argues, "the Negro cries Amen! and swears that to so much of this strange prejudice as is founded on just homage to civilization, culture, righteousness, and progress, he humbly bows and meekly does obeisance."[10] Thus, the civil rights era appears as an anomaly, bookended by periods of Black embrace of the status quo in the form of moral and religious principles. Unimpeachable values become the discursive form of the repression of collective action, rather than its catalyst.

Hence, Harris's model provides a lucid explanation for one facet of the link between social discourse and collective action, but it does not tell the whole story. It may be possible to invoke religious discourse as a catalyst to collective action at certain historical periods, but the model cannot provide a link between the change in public discourse and the lapse in Black collective action. Nor can we make much progress by extending Harris's argument to other types of "everyday talk," as Melissa Harris-Lacewell did in *Barbershops, Bibles, and BET*. There is ample empirical and theoretical evidence, particularly from the field of ethnography, supporting the claim that Blacks' discussions in church and at the barbershop influence their political opinions, among which is a belief in what they see as "persistent social and economic inequality" and the view that such inequality can be overcome by individualism and integration with White society.[11] This, however, is insufficient to take us out of the barbershop and into the streets.

THE PSYCHOLOGY OF EBULLIENCE

Collective action is lacking in today's Black community, owing in part to paradoxical ebullience, which exists despite strong non-elite avenues of communication. We must, therefore, hypothesize that Black ebullience, or the tendency to adopt attitudes expressed in elite discourse in spite of social evidence, serves an important psychological purpose. Research into the question of a disconnect between Black perceptions of racism today is thus closely related to research into the role that the experience of discrimination and racism has had on the psychological health of Blacks. This line of research looks for buffers that blunt the impact of external racist experience, so Blacks can still feel good about themselves. Mia Smith Bynum, Candace Best, Sandra L. Barnes, and E. Thomoseo Burton, for example, investigated how private regard, Blacks' feelings about themselves and about being Black, reduced the effect of racism on internalizing symptoms.[12] They found that Black males with higher private regard were able to use their optimism as a strength to blunt the impact of racist experiences and to control the anxiety and depression symptoms resulting from experiences of racism, "Feeling positive about being African American and holding positive attitudes towards other African Americans can serve to reduce the harmful effects of racism."[13]

Racism is known to lead to psychological health problems in Blacks, but the painful effects of racism may be reduced if Blacks view themselves, in their Blackness, in a positive light. One piece of the puzzle in explaining ebullience, therefore, is that it serves to help Blacks maintain their own psychological well-being. Evidence about the lack of social progress (a notion which is problematic in itself, as we have seen) does not overcome the emotional necessity of remaining positive about the Black community.

This phenomenon also suggests a mechanism by which, over time, strong private regard may serve to reinforce color-blind narratives in Blacks of high self-esteem. Nevertheless, Blacks continue to have lower levels of trust in the government, so it remains unclear how this psychological aspect of ebullience connects to elite racial discourse. Donald P. Haider-Markel, William Delehanty, and Matthew Beverlin provide a clue.[14] They address the problem of Black attitudes toward race in today's America from the perspective of media theory, which is directly relevant to our interest in discourse. The media's response to Hurricane Katrina in 2005 focused on Blacks' negative views of the government response to the disaster. This corresponded to poll results, which showed a wide split between Whites and Blacks regarding attitudes about government responses. Haider-Markel et al. argue that, by covering stories of Blacks unhappy with the response, the media may have racialized the event, leading Blacks to adopt less positive attitudes as a result of the media's framing. The images of Black victims "very likely made the average black viewer feel more affinity toward the victims than viewers of other races."[15] Alexander Czopp and Margo Monteith also posit that media framing and positive stereotyping could influence black self-perception for psychological reasons, independently of social realities.[16] Positive or benevolent racism toward Blacks, consisting of positive stereotypes, could play a role in reducing Black awareness of the presence of racism.

This same identification may be at work in the Obama era,

when elite discourse about Blacks is increasingly coming from Blacks themselves. If, as media theory suggests, Blacks identify with others of their own race, they may be more likely to accept the narratives of Black progress and ebullience when they come from Black elites themselves. Thus, the media framing of Obama's 2008 candidacy, which accepted Obama's rhetoric regarding the emergence of a post-racial America, may have accounted for the development of positive perceptions of race among Blacks. Furthermore, when Blacks see or hear of other Blacks who have become successful, they identify with those images of success, believing themselves, individually and collectively, to be more successful relative to Whites. These perceptions, because they serve an important psychological and emotional purpose, have the power to overcome statistics regarding socioeconomic disparities. Thus, the complex dynamic between discourse and political action is strongly influenced by the everyday psychology of race.

THE CIRCULAR DYNAMIC OF DISCOURSE AND ACTION

The dissemination of alternative political viewpoints and the drive for collective action are merely the starting point of a more complex dynamic through which discourse and action are mutually reinforcing given the correct psychological and emotional climate. President Obama in his commencement address at Morehouse College, stated, "Nobody cares if you suffered some discrimination. . . . You have to remember that whatever you've gone through, it pales in comparison to the hardships previous generations endured. . . . And if they overcame them, you can overcome them, too."[17] Thus, we see a successful, elite Black male encouraging self-reliance and private regard and minimizing the psychological effects of racism. This is a powerful combination: the audience identifies with an exemplar of Black success, hears him insisting that their situation is greatly improved compared to that of previous generations, and receives an everyday psychological benefit from remaining optimistic. Not only is collective action discouraged, the emotional and psychological impetus to collective action is removed, and even the rational motivation (i.e., the lack of equality) is denied at the level of elite discourse. Given all this, it is perhaps unsurprising that social statistics do not lead to more outrage in today's Black community.

Stephen Ellingson forcefully argued for something like this complex understanding of collective action. According to this view, the link between discourse and action is circular, rather than linear (as Harris had supposed). Public argumentation, such as that found in the Black church of the civil rights era, can spur collective action, but discourse only becomes broadly compelling *after* collective action has begun.[18] Protests, for example, provide the evidence that political and religious leaders need to legitimate or discredit social movements. (Incidentally, Ellingson lists "taking a morally or politically unassailable position" as one of the key discursive strategies for discrediting collective action—a strategy we have seen both before and after civil rights, such that "the Negro cries Amen!" in the face of oppression.[19]) We might, then, view the first nonviolent actions of the civil rights era as direct results of the ideas spread at the level of local churches; however, the Movement could not have gained broad support without those first actions that had the effect of generating public interest in the Black struggle, providing visible support for the claims King and other Black leaders were advancing. Hence I conclude that discourse initiates action, which strengthens discourse, thereby initiating action on a larger scale.

This dialectical model gives us an explanation of the shift from the collective action of the civil rights and Black Power eras to the individualistic orientation of today. Whereas we may be able to find isolated instances of discourse supporting collective Black identity and supporting continued struggle for economic emancipation, this discursive trend has been unable to catalyze the events necessary to bring broad awareness and support to this effort. From here it seems like a short step to the conclusion that high-profile individualist discourse (Barack Obama) and academic dismissal of collectivism (John McWhorter) have simply outweighed their opposite, acting as a dampening force that has prevented collective action from catalyzing to a sufficient degree. However, we must still inquire into the mechanism behind this effect. Does individualist discourse discourage collective action from the outset, or does it reframe existing collective action, giving such action a negative meaning around which Black identity is therefore prevented from crystallizing?

RESPONDING TO ACTION: THE POST-RACIAL DISCURSIVE LANDSCAPE

I now shift my focus back, once and for all, to our post-racial era. So far, this chapter has established that everyday discourse, including local conversations and Black media, can influence Blacks' political opinions and voting records, but that such discourse is not enough to lead to large-scale change through collective action. In addition, it is necessary that discourse spur local action and that the establishment *respond* to this action in a way that reinforces discourse and legitimates future action. In the post-racial era, such a response is all but absent. Indeed, the establishment response has been to condemn and *de*legitimate collective action, encouraging self-empowerment within the existing order as an alternative.

One particularly salient example of this is the role of religious institutions in distributing social welfare at the community level. In *God and Government in the Ghetto*, Michael Owens reveals how this dynamic functions.[20] Government grants and social programs—ostensibly intended to improve living conditions, economic opportunity, and social cohesion in poor Black neighborhoods—are disseminated by church organizations under the auspices of activist collaboration. Proponents of this system, including Owens himself, argue that church collaboration in welfare programs lends Black clergy a degree of political influence that they otherwise would not enjoy. Owing to their connections in offices of power and public agencies, church leaders can contribute to the direction of policy and give voice to the concerns of the Black community. However, in line with the prevailing trend, Owens was overly optimistic. In fact, there is reason to suppose that the direction of power and influence proceeds down to Black community churches, rather than upward to the level of policy. Members of the clergy, if they hope to continue receiving monetary benefits, are not likely to encourage active dissent. Thus the religious motivation[21] to quell dissent is joined by a political motivation, further entrenching anticollectivist discourse and disseminating individualist ideas from the elite level down to the grass roots.

Emerging research continues to confirm this hypothesis—that the post-racial Black church serves as a gatekeeper, condemning collective action and framing Black linked fate as an outmoded idea. Amandia Speakes-Lewis, Leroy L. Gill, and Crystal George Moses provided one cogent analysis of the shift away from collectivism in the Black church, which they attribute to the trend of mega-churches and the consumerization of religion: "In this post-modern era, where the Black church has adopted the cultural habits of the dominant society, we are witnessing a radical departure from rich heritage that was bequeathed to a people that gain glory in solidarity to community. . . . Today, prosperity preaching appears to foster a preoccupation with . . . individual profit."[22] A similar trend has been observed in the political and news media. Riva Brown conducted a content analysis of media framing strategies used in response to the 2012 shooting of Black teen Trayvon Martin by a White/Hispanic male. Fascinatingly, although the shooting was framed as driven by fear and racism, Brown showed that the media channeled public outrage away from social racism and toward issues of voter suppression and voting rights. Additionally, Black establishment organizations like the National Association for the Advancement of Colored People (NAACP), which organized marches and rallies following the acquittal of Martin's murderer, failed to secure news coverage of these events and did not encourage its supporters to engage in collective action to address the concerns that the incident raised.[23] This is a clear example of how collective action, even when spurred by organized discourse, can fail to raise social awareness and create change if it is not followed in its turn by intensified and widely distributed discourse.

Finally, we can trace these social and political phenomena, which lead to failures of discourse that suppress action, through to the Black politics of today. As I showed in the previous chapter, thinkers like Andra Gillespie have identified a tendency for successful Black leaders to distance themselves from concerns of Black identity, catering to the White establishment and embracing individualism. Indeed, as Gillespie has it, *only* Black politicians who adhere to this program are granted entrance into the political elite. Today, the rise of the Black right closely follows Gillespie's arguments. Although there have always been conservative Black politicians, the twenty-first century has seen, for the first time since the transition en masse of the Black voter base to the Democrat party, the rise of a prominent Black constituency on the right. What distinguishes politicians like Ben Carson, Herman Cain, and Allen West from their Democrat counterparts is precisely their willingness to distance themselves from the history of Black politics and Black identity. Herman Cain, in particular, was outspoken in opposition to the prophetic religious tradition that has long characterized the Black church, placing himself in a direct contrast to Martin Luther King Jr. and others. As Charles Henry argues, "the concept of 'deracialization' has served as a form of accommodationism that encourages Black political actors to emphasize policy issues with broad cross-racial appeal."[24] Even Barack

Obama, in his 2008 presidential campaign, portrayed himself as an integrated member of the American "melting pot," glorifying integration and condemning the formation of group identity.

CONCLUSION: MOVING PAST THE "OBAMA EFFECT"

All these disparate threads of the argument come together to support the central conclusion that the prominence of individualist rhetoric constitutes a negative reaction to collective action that discourages broad movements from taking root. Whereas, during the civil rights–era collective action was supported and legitimated both by the media and in Black everyday talk, the post-racial era has seen a redirection, reframing, and thus quelling of such action. The result, as we have seen, has been the view that collective action is the expression of degeneracy and that optimism, what I have termed paradoxical ebullience, is the righteous response to Blacks' individual and collective concerns. Thus, again, the prevailing view that Black optimism is attributable to the "Obama effect"[25] proves too simplistic. The simple fact of a Black president is far overshadowed by the political, social, and discursive reality in which that president was elected. Black optimism has become an instrument of White oppression. Deracialized Black elites in the religious, political, and social arenas advance discourse of color-blind ideology and preach the value of individual effort, equality, and self-help.

In summary, there is evidence to suggest a connection between social knowledge and Blacks' socioeconomic situation. Economic statistics indicate that the latter remains in a state of stagnation. Therefore, we must look to the former for new avenues to change that can realign Black attitudes with Black socioeconomic realities.

CHAPTER 5

Black America at the End of the Obama Era

I have presented my analysis showing that Black socioeconomic ebullience and individualistic attitudes are influenced
by discourse and have the effect of diminishing Black collective action to address socioeconomic stagnation. A decline in
linked fate and collective action jeopardizes policies that provide socioeconomic benefits to Blacks. In the absence of a social
movement to reverse these trends, race conscious universal policy solutions may be a strategic way to address these problems.[1]

Paradoxical ebullience contributes to the elimination of socioeconomic policies through a disempowered sense of linked fate
among Blacks. We have seen that ebullience and individualism
are associated with a loss of Black belief in linked fate and collective action to lobby for the group's parity. In the light of continued reversal of race-conscious policies, the racial wealth gap
and other socioeconomic gaps are likely to continue to stagnate
or widen.[2] The unfortunate conclusion to which all this leads
is that elite Black discourse has led, not to a liberation of the
Black public through individual empowerment (as Obama and
McWhorter have perhaps hoped), but to a resurgence of structural racism made possible by the widespread abandonment of
collective action. However, thanks largely to advances in technology, the one-to-one correspondence between themes present
in elite discourse and public sentiment is no longer a foregone
conclusion. A new form of discourse has become possible with
the rise of social media, and, at the end of Obama's presidency,

it was already becoming clear that this new discourse had the potential to open new possibilities for social change and forward movement.

BLACK LIVES MATTER AND A NEW KIND OF HOPE

The rise of social media has already complicated the issues discussed in this book, pointing the way forward to a new kind of hope for change that is not, perhaps, entirely dependent on public policy. In the wake of the deaths of Trayvon Martin, Eric Garner, and Troy Davis in the early 2010s, a new kind of non-elite discourse arose, largely on the social media site Twitter. A subset of Twitter users referred to as "Black Twitter" uses the site to advocate for sociopolitical change. Hashtags like "#BlackLivesMatter" provided a way for ordinary Blacks to express their outrage at what they viewed as racist reactions and manifestations of systemic injustices on the part of police forces and legal systems across the country. This movement sparked a new, passionate discussion of race in the United States that began to question elite, color-blind discourse. In at least one case, the movement led to action to convict perpetrators of violence. However, some social justice and civil rights advocates see Black Lives Matter as a failed movement that has not yet resulted in sweeping change.[3]

At the level of elite politics, President Obama supported the Black Lives Matter movement, defending it against critics' claims that the movement is antipolice or aggressive. In February 2016, Obama convened a panel to discuss the problems facing the Black community with Black Lives Matter organizers and established civil rights leaders. This was a positive development, indicating that elites like Obama were willing to consider ways in which their individualist rhetoric may not be meeting the needs of Black communities. It also suggested a resurgence of interest in collective action at a national level among young

Blacks. However, not all observers viewed these developments in a positive light. Some viewed Obama's gesture to Black Lives Matter activists as mere lip service, insisting that the government sought to send the false impression that it intended to work for the causes important to activists.[4] Other commentators argued that, "even by Obama standards, the president seemed to react to the shooting of an unarmed black man and the subsequent anger with unusual caution. Obama expressed his distress about the incident, but he also pleaded for calm and chastised those who rioted—a reaction that devastated many African-Americans, who thought he was emphasizing the stereotype of black lawlessness."[5] As Obama's presidency was drawing to a close, there was no consensus about Obama's effect on racial politics in the United States. Everyone agreed that race issues in this country are complex and that Obama had difficulty enacting many changes that he would have liked to have seen become reality. His presidency was a historical landmark, but it escalated racial tensions, drawing a stark contrast to the rhetoric of a post-racial society that was so in vogue after Obama's election in 2008.[6]

It remains to be seen whether Black Lives Matter and similar movements can result in long-lasting national policy change that persists even through opposing political regimes like that of Donald Trump. Its importance at this stage is in establishing a new form of non-elite discourse with the potential to counter official narratives of power, unite communities around uncomfortable ideas, and provide social and psychological support for those ideas. Social media has the potential to obviate the psychological necessity, described in the previous chapter, of paradoxical ebullience. Nationwide movements like Black Lives Matter introduce a new possibility for being Black, by which Blacks can maintain private regard and self-esteem in their racial status while still confronting and addressing the social problems facing the Black community. New media like Twitter may be replacing Black leadership in the dynamic of collective action. The Black community may not need a new Martin Luther King Jr. or a new Malcolm X to lead them into action. They can self-collectivize under new identity labels like Black Twitter.

Interestingly, some commentators have minimized the Black Lives Matter movement, in keeping with their ideological commitments. For example, expanding on comments he made in an interview with CNN, John McWhorter, proponent of the idea of Black self-sabotage, gave a dismissive analysis of the movement. "Fighting only for the Black lives that are taken by Whites is arbitrary," he said, suggesting that race is unimportant in the quest to reduce police brutality. Here we see starkly the difference between McWhorter's post-racialism and post-Blackness as an approach to race that might take a more realistic approach to racial issues within the criminal justice system as a whole. McWhorter also suggested that Black-on-Black crime was a more serious problem and spoke dismissively of conversations about interracial tension.[7] Given the spontaneity, youthful energy, and viral appeal of the Black Lives Matter movement, McWhorter's comments sound woefully out of touch.

Fredrick Harris, among others, pointed out an irony in the timing of the movement: "That's one of the fundamental paradoxes of Obama's presidency—that we have the Black Lives Matter movement under a black president. Your man is in office, and you have this whole movement around criminal-justice reform asserting black people's humanity?"[8] Russell Rickford of Cornell University made some useful strides toward explaining this seemingly paradoxical resurgence of Black protest under a Black president. First, he noted, civil rights leaders and activists experienced "political paralysis and isolation" during the Obama presidency, leading to disappointment with the gains made under Obama and a renewed interest in "confrontation politics."[9]

However, as Rickford himself pointed out, Black Lives Matter activists are young, and most are not full-time organizers or activists. It may be, therefore, that the partial success of the Occupy Wall Street movement, which focused on income inequality, laid the groundwork for Black Lives Matter by reminding the Black community, ironically outside the context of racial discourse, of the potential social efficacy of mass movements. The failure of a Black president to justify Black optimism by effecting visible socioeconomic change may have helped to awaken Blacks from the trance of individualism. Indeed, many of the racist criminal justice policies at issue in the Black Lives Matter movement began or continued under Obama. This may be a new paradox, but one with the potential to lead us forward from the paradox of ebullience.

Historically, paradoxes are often not overcome or resolved per se. Rather, they are dissolved, rendered logically possible, and reconciled by newly emergent possibilities. Earlier, in chapter 1, we saw that the theory of post-Blackness, while flawed, is one such attempt at a new possibility of thinking about race. Rather than succumbing to a false dichotomy between "racial" and "post-racial," the idea of post-Blackness both embraces race at a systemic level, acknowledging its importance to everyday social realities, and eschews its importance as a collective identity, asserting that all individual ways of being Black are equally valid and authentic. As we have seen in the foregoing analysis, collective identity may be more important to the future of Blacks in the United States than the post-Black agenda suggests. However, the basic impulse of deconstructing limiting binaries appears to be having a real effect, as the Black Lives Matter movement demonstrates. Rather than simply accepting that Blacks must *either* be optimistic *or* take collective action to change the status quo, this emerging Black public can be seen as rejecting the mutual exclusivity of the old paradigm.

If the trends suggested by the Black Lives Matter movement continue, we may see a dissolution of the paradox of ebullience in the face of alarming social realities. Instead, through the use of new media tools, Blacks may come to frame their own experience of race as an ebullient one, working together for action and change and thereby creating a new reality that justifies ebullience. Without the socioeconomic and justice disparities at issue in the Black Lives Matter movement, the movement could not exist. Yet it is precisely movements like this one that legitimate and make consistent the Black community's ebullience and hope for the future.

Although the non-elite discourse made possible by social media is now undisputedly an essential force for change, Black Lives Matter and similar movements will need to form alliances with elites in order to translate shifts in public awareness into shifts in policy and, ultimately, in socioeconomic reality. What Black Lives Matter demonstrates is that the Black public now has the power to overcome and, if necessary, undermine elite discourse, crafting narratives of its own that are not localized in particular offices or positions of power but that exist independently of the many individuals who propound them. During the 2016 presidential election, for example, the movement was responsible for shifting the discourse surrounding the candidacies of Democrats Hillary Clinton and Bernie Sanders, often through unsanctioned disruption at political rallies. What remains to be seen is how, without an attachment to elite offices of power, this new non-elite discourse can effect the kind of broad, lasting change that the United States still needs in order to end the trauma of racism.

RACE CONSCIOUS UNIVERSAL POLICY RECOMMENDATIONS

One effect of post-racial rhetoric is the inaccurate framing of Black socioeconomic stagnation as a failure of Blacks to capitalize on opportunities generated by the civil rights movement, rather than as a result of the intractability of structural racism. This leads elites to address racial disparity with recourse to austerity measures or a policy framework grounded in behavioral mod-ification.[10] In response to this, some scholars recognize the need for race-conscious universal policies for all Americans, leading to economic stability for the most disparate.[11] Such policies should consider the accumulated and continuing effects of structural rac-ism as well as the racial dynamism of policy creation.[12] As Alberto Alesina, Edward Glaeser, and Bruce Sacerdote explain, welfare state capitalism is not feasible given the demographic diversity of the United States.[13] These authors noted that Eurocentric nations, in contrast to the racially diverse United States, have historically demographic homogeneity. This European homogeneity makes it possible to support redistribution policies; however, the stark racial heterogeneity and "racial animosity in the U.S. makes redis-tribution to the poor, who are disproportionately black, unappeal-ing to many voters."[14] In the light of this racial heterogeneity and animosity, policymakers should consider ways to implement poli-cies that account for racial differences in socioeconomic outcomes.

My analysis, too, suggests that the use of race-targeted policies has currently evolved to be politically impractical for addressing disparate socioeconomic outcomes among Blacks. It would be more advantageous to advance policies that boldly target areas in which Blacks experience disproportionately neg-ative outcomes, such as socioeconomic progress. According to Theda Skocpol, targeted universal policy solutions "redistrib-ute income and deliver special services to certain groups of dis-advantaged Americans without risking public disaffection."[15] Targeted universalism as a mechanism of redistribution may be better received than policies that are viewed as earmark pro-grams, especially if those programs become racialized. Another proponent of targeted universalism, john powell, promotes interventions that are focused on the needs of everyone, but pay special attention to the needs of the most disenfranchised.[16] Skocpol and powell part company where targeted universal-ism intersects with outcomes; in powell's assessment, targeted universalism ignores racism. Looking at real racial disparities, powell admonished policymakers to acknowledge the existence and insidiousness of structural racism, engage with it in a manner that does not further marginalize individuals, and assess policies by their outcomes, not their intents.

An example of a race-conscious universal policy that focuses on both intent *and* outcome is Darity and Hamilton's "baby bond" policy.[17] These authors provide a way forward to bridge the racial socioeconomic gap that goes beyond private action and market forces, which are not sufficient.[18] Darity and Hamilton state that the answer lies in public sector resources in the form of federal government distributions of seed money to give marginalized individuals access to assets that will appreciate; this is particularly important, they argued, for those born into families at the low end of the wealth distribution. These authors propose a "baby bond" with graduated endowments for children based on familial net worth. The authors estimated the cost for this program to be 2.2 percent of 2012 federal expenditure, or $80 billion, and emphasized that the cost to bridge the unjust racial wealth gap is negligible to the federal government. Furthermore, the authors argued that their proposal would be more equitable than the current government spending on asset development. To illustrate, the Corporation for Enterprise Development and the Annie E. Casey Foundation in 2010 estimated that in 2009 the federal government earmarked $400 billion in tax subsidies to sponsor asset development policies, and, of this allocation, more than half of it benefited those who earned over $160,000 per year. Those in the bottom 60 percent only received 4 percent of the benefit.

Another example of a race-conscious universal policy would be a federal job guarantee. This policy, as articulated by Alan Aja et al., would offer job security for all Americans, helping to close the persistent racial unemployment gap. The authors claimed that such a policy would ultimately address the disproportionate bargaining power between capital and labor by removing the threat of unemployment for all workers.[19]

These innovative policies may help address the problems faced by Black Americans, but they will not be enough. In addition to race-conscious universal policies, a collective political and ideological movement to counteract the post-racial normative trend to help Blacks better advocate for policies to affect the group's economic outcomes may be necessary, as is new leadership to guide the movement. The extent to which Blacks share in available economic, social, and political resources remains disproportionately low compared with their presence in the general population, as indicated by the racial wealth and income gaps.[20]

CONCLUSION

Paradoxical ebullience is a new contribution to socioeconomic theory and practice. This theory characterizes extreme optimism despite economic stagnation, which diminishes Blacks' collective will to both address socioeconomic stagnation and lobby for policies that provide them with socioeconomic parity. It is worth reiterating that elites maintain the status quo of Black socioeconomic marginalization through discourse structures rooted in contemporary theories of color blindness, laissez-faire racism, and post-racialism. These theories standardize Black socioeconomic disadvantage as the result of Blacks' failure to be industrious, responsible individuals who work hard and take responsibility for their success.

While it is true that Black identity has expanded beyond race, the intragroup differences are much smaller than intergroup differences with Whites, at least where socioeconomic parity is concerned. In short, race is far more salient in influencing life chances for Blacks' than any other cleavages that make Blacks different from one another. Despite this, post-racial discourse leads Blacks to abandon collective action as a means to make socioeconomic gains. All this leaves Blacks with a deracialized political process that is unable to rectify racially influenced political outcomes.

As Chief Justice Roberts said when he wrote for the majority in *Shelby County v. Holder*, the legislation Congress enacts to fix discrimination in voting rights needs to address current conditions, especially the erroneous assumption that discrimination against minorities to exercise their right to vote is not widespread. It is paradoxical to use normative, value-based policies to address objective conditions of Black socioeconomic stagnation. It is also paradoxical to do this and to expect Blacks to achieve socioeconomic parity. Therefore, policymakers should look at the current, objective evidence, relative and absolute, regarding Black socioeconomic standing, such as the racial unemployment gap and the racial wealth gap. Policymakers and the resulting policy enactment on Black socioeconomic stagnation should also take into account the empirical evidence relating to Blacks' long-term participation in the opportunities of a putative post-racial society—evidence that demonstrates that Blacks, on average, have more educational attainment than Whites, after controlling for family background.[21] This evidence suggests that Blacks are not disenchanted with education but rather are interested in doing well academically like their White peers.[22] It also suggests that Whites are no more frugal than Blacks when it comes to saving money.[23] As we have seen, it is disingenuous for policymakers to emphasize maladaptive values and behaviors on the part of Blacks and minimize the role of structural racism against Blacks and the resulting impact on their life chances.

Having begun with the election of Barack Obama, which coincided with the upsurge in Black optimism that motivated this book, it seems natural to conclude with the end of his presidency. In his farewell address, President Obama began by reaffirming his belief in self-determination, with a nod to collectivism taking second place: he lauded "the freedom to chase our individual dreams through our sweat and toil and imagination, and the imperative to strive together, as well, to achieve a common good, a greater good." As the address went on, however, the tone shifted. Obama repeatedly used the word *solidarity,* a word charged with undertones of political activism, suggesting that the nation's founders "knew that democracy does require a basic sense of solidarity—the idea that for all our outward differences, we're all in this together; that we rise or fall as one." Obama's suggestion that we ignore our "outward differences" may have been intended as a comment on the divisions of political partisanship, but seems highly relevant in the context of race. Later, when Obama turned explicitly to the issue of race, he acknowledged the racial tension that had divided the country during his second term in office, but did not waver in his optimism and post-racial discourse: "Race relations are better than they were 10, or 20, or 30 years ago, no matter what some folks say," and, "Regardless of the station that we occupy, we all have to try harder. . . . If every economic issue is framed as a struggle between a hardworking white middle class and an undeserving minority, then workers of all shades are going to be left fighting for scraps while the wealthy withdraw further into their private enclaves."[24]

These statements, for better or worse, solidified Obama's legacy as the post-racial, individualist Black president. Addressing paradoxical ebullience and closing the gap between Blacks' racial attitudes about their socioeconomic parity and their actual socioeconomic outcomes will require a new kind of rhetoric on the part of Obama's Black elite successors. Elite discourse must reflect Blacks' socioeconomic reality, come together with the new non-elite discourse (e.g., Black Lives Matter), and advocate for policies that provide economic access and stability for Black Americans. There *is,* paradoxically, room for optimism that the new social movements can shift the consciousness of policy to align elite and non-elite discourse in moving forward.

The Role of Elite Discourse in the Trump Era and Beyond

As I prepare this book to go to press, I cannot pass over Donald Trump's presidency in silence. It would be easy enough to decry the more-prominent-than-ever racism of the far right, many of whom are Trump supporters. Indeed, social and mainstream media are overfull with such accusations, which there would be little point in my reiterating them here. Instead, I would like to offer some remarks focusing specifically on the marriage between elite rhetoric and public opinion, which has been my focus from the outset. As we shall see, the Trump presidency constitutes strong evidence that the traditional role of elite discourse in American society has given way to a new, more collective, and distributed non-elite discourse that is fundamentally altering how elite discourse functions and how public opinion emerges and shifts.

Michael Dawson noted that collective action tends to increase when the opposition party is in power; since most Blacks are Democrats, we expect to see a rise in organizing in the Black community during the Republican Trump administration.[1] But we might expect the mechanism of this rise in organizing to involve opposition rhetoric: the more the party in power speaks out against the issues that affect the Black community, the more the Black community perceives that the Republican government does not actively support its interests, and the more collective action increases as a response to an increased sense of disenfranchisement. During the Democratic Obama presidency, individualist rhetoric seemed to have the effect of decreasing the impulse to collective action, supporting this hypothesis. The Trump era, however, begins to tell a different story. The renewed sense of urgency to race politics coincides with the perception of the Republican Party as the opposition party, but it seems to break with the notion that the party's rhetoric is responsible. The content of the campaign rhetoric of candidate Trump and his administration's early discourse (of which I will give several concrete examples below) has been characterized by numerous overtures to Blacks, some of which might even be characterized as supporting the notion of linked fate by focusing on the community more than on individual actions. This rhetorical stance is, given the traditionally individualist ideology of the Republican Party, somewhat unexpected, as is the Black community's refusal to buy into the rhetoric.

To understand why, we need to look at the specific form this rhetoric has taken by reviewing several exemplars. Given the ongoing nature of these events, it is difficult to draw any firm conclusions, and it is not my place here to attempt to predict the future, which will inevitably be the past by the time this book reaches your hands. What I would like to emphasize, with the following remarks constituting just one example, is the importance of stepping back from individual discursive acts, extricating ourselves from the scandalous reportage in which they are often enmeshed, and holding them in view long enough to see the patterns that begin to emerge. In so doing, we can disabuse ourselves of theories and assumptions that, while functional for past eras and under old circumstances, no longer serve us in our quest to understand the American public. To this end, we will benefit, first, from taking stock of a few prominent rhetorical "moments" of the Trump era so far.

- As candidate for the presidency, Donald Trump emphasized Black-on-Black violence, citing as an example the unprecedented levels of violence affecting Black neighborhoods in Chicago. Famously, Trump described conditions in Black urban communities as bleak, with poor education, high unemployment, and epidemic gun violence. Although Trump's supporters read these comments as an attempt to reach out to the Black community, many Blacks were unconvinced. Many suggested that Trump's comments ignored the tumultuous history of the Black race in America. President Obama sarcastically criticized Trump, saying that he had, "missed that whole civics lesson about slavery or Jim Crow."[2]

- During Trump's campaign, a gunman killed five police officers at a Black Lives Matter march in Dallas, Texas. Trump took the opportunity to emphasize the need for "law and order" and the need to stabilize communities.[3] Later, soon after his inauguration (after winning only 8 percent of the Black vote), President Trump renewed his commitment to law and order, condemning what he called the "anti-police atmosphere" in the United States. Some saw this as an indirect warning to the Black Lives Matter movement, implying that the administration would take the side of law enforcement in any discussion of systemic racism in police forces.[4]

- At a "listening session" organized at the White House for Black History Month, President Trump made the following remark, "Frederick Douglass is an example of somebody who's done an amazing job and is being recognized more and more, I notice."[5] Critics suggested, based on his phrasing, that Trump may not have known who Frederick Douglass was. At the same meeting, Trump reiterated his law-and-order stance on Black communities: "We need safer communities, and we're going to do that with law enforcement."[6]

- Later the same month, President Trump's secretary of education, Betsy DeVos, issued a statement in which she referred to historically Black colleges and universities (HBCUs) as "pioneers when it comes to school choice." The statement was widely viewed as disingenuous and insensitive, failing to acknowledge the origin of HBCUs, rooted in Jim Crow–era segregation.[7]

- A week after DeVos's statement, Ben Carson, the secretary of Housing and Urban Development (HUD), gave a speech to HUD employees in which he focused on the American mythos as a land of opportunity for immigrants. In the speech, he passingly described African slaves as immigrants, and the comparison, the words of a *New York Times* reporter, "was met with swift outrage online."[8]

- Alveda King, the niece of Martin Luther King Jr., praised Donald Trump's record on race relations in an interview with Fox News.[9] Around the same time, the Congressional Black Caucus (CBC), a group of Black lawmakers at the federal level, released a list of one hundred "racially problematic" actions that President Trump had taken during his first one hundred days in office. The list focused particularly on proposed budget cuts for social programs, including the Minority Business Development Agency and the Department of Housing and Urban Development. It also referenced the administration's "divisive and tone-deaf rhetoric."[10]

- Around a month later, the CBC refused Trump's invitation to meet to discuss race relations in America. In a public statement, the CBC stated that it had received little response from Trump's administration to the numerous letters it had written expressing concerns about the effect of Trump's policies on Black America: "We have seen no evidence that your administration acted on our calls for action, and we have in fact witnessed steps that will affirmatively hurt Black communities."[11]

- At the level of non-elite discourse, Twitter and other social media continue to play an important role in race relations and in establishing the concept of a Black community in

the United States. Although the Black Lives Matter movement remains a prominent influence, popular hashtags like
"#StayWoke," referring to the necessity to keep informed
about political developments relevant to the community,
emerge as temporary notions around which discourse can
congeal. The CBC used the already popular hashtag to promote its comments.[12]

It is clear from the examples above that neither Black elites
nor everyday Blacks are prepared to accept rhetorical overtures
to the community like those the Trump administration has
repeatedly attempted. Indeed, even elite Blacks like Alveda
King and Kanye West have been criticized by the Black community for their support for or even affiliation with Donald Trump.

In terms of linked fate, this is a very different picture than
the one we saw at the beginning of the Obama administration.
Although, eight years prior to Trump's election, a common
Black identity was evident in polling and research results, it was
mostly kept quiet. The open discussion of Black identity, Black
community, and Black progress represents a real shift. Whether
this shift was brought about primarily by the disappointments
of the Obama era or by the perceived threats of the Trump era,
we may never be able to discern. What is clear, however, is that
the conceptual foundation necessary for collective action is
increasingly solid.

However much the beneficiaries of the twenty-four-hour news
cycle may encourage us to forget last week's outrages or last
year's policy conundrums, we should resist the temptation.
Only by taking a longer view of discourse, as I have attempted
to do with Obama's speeches in this book, can we gain a true
understanding of the how and why we think the way we do.

This book began with a public opinion poll, so it is appropriate at the close to return to the question of how public opinion
has shifted. In 2010, the same year a Pew poll showed Black
optimism at a high, Gallup found that just over 10 percent of

Americans said they worried "a great deal" about race relations, an all time low since polling began for that statistic.[13] By 2016, that number had shot up to an astounding 35 percent. A 2016 Pew poll found that 45 percent of Whites and 61 percent of Blacks thought that race relations in the United States were "generally bad."[14]

I see this change as a strong argument for the power of social media. Despite the individualist discourse of President Obama and other prominent Black elites, the individualist mindset experienced a swift decline, coinciding exactly with the rise of the Black Lives Matter movement. Later, despite apparently conciliatory rhetoric on the part of Republicans, the Black community, driven largely by social media and by the mainstream media's reporting of social media trends, has redoubled its expressions of outrage. We live, therefore, in an age where ideas, rather than individuals, are the drivers of public opinion. We look, as the CBC did, beyond words, to the *actions* of those in power to determine whether we can trust them and count on their support. And we who live outside of elite circles use social media as a way of "crowd-sourcing" our interpretations of those actions. Mainstream media outlets also play a role here by reporting and, thereby, reinforcing such interpretations. Whereas reporters once played a primary interpretive role, they now act largely as aggregators of bottom-up analysis on the part of influential members of the general public.

What patterns will emerge when we begin to take seriously, aggregate, and analyze prominent units of non-elite discourse? A new type of analysis may be the key to untangling the social and political situations that appear nonsensical when we apply the tools of traditional discourse analysis. When elite discourse no longer matters in the same way it once did, we need inventive ways to discern what *does* matter for understanding public opinion and its paradoxes.

NOTES

Introduction: The Paradoxical Ebullience Problem

1. Pew Research Center, *Blacks Upbeat about Black Progress, Prospects* (Washington, DC: Pew Research Center, 2010), http://www.pewsocialtrends
.org/2010/01/12/blacks-upbeat-about-black-progress-prospects/, pars. 3–12.
2. William Darity Jr. and Darrick Hamilton, "Bold Policies for Economic Justice," *Review of Black Political Economy* 39, no. 1 (2012): 79–85.
3. Ibid., 80.
4. Rebecca Tippet, Avis Jones-DeWeever, Maya Rockeymoore, Darrick Hamilton, and William Darity Jr., *Beyond Broke: Why Closing the Racial Wealth Gap is a Priority for National Economic Security* (Report prepared by Center for Global Policy Solutions and The Research Network on Ethnic and Racial Inequality at Duke University with funds provided by the Ford Foundation, 2014), http://globalpolicysolutions.org/wp
-content/uploads/2014/04/BeyondBroke_Exec_Summary.pdf, 4.
5. Alan S. Gerber and Gregory A. Huber, "Partisanship, Political Control, and Economic Assessments," *American Journal of Political Science* 54, no. 1 (2010): 153–173; Gheorghe H. Popescu, "Partisan Differences in Evaluations of the Economy," *Economics, Management, and Financial Markets* 8, no. 1 (2013): 130–35.
6. Pew Research Center, "A Deep Dive into Party Affiliation: Sharp Differences by Race, Gender, Generation, Education," http://www.people-press.org/2015/04/07/a-deep-dive-into-party-affiliation/, par. 5.
7. I use the terms *individualist* and *collectivist* to refer to the belief that Blacks' own hard work and responsibility result in their socioeconomic gains and the belief that Black gains are the result of a group or collective effort, respectively.
8. Robert Bernasconi and Tommy L. Lott, eds. *The Idea of Race* (Indianapolis, IN: Hackett, 2000), 1–2.
9. Georges Louis-Leclerc, Comte de Buffon, *Natural History, General and*

Particular, vol. III. 2nd ed., trans. William Smellie (London: W. Strahan and T. Cadell, 1785), 197.

10. Immanuel Kant, "Of the Different Races of Men," in *Race and the Enlightenment: A Reader*, ed. Emmanuel Chukwudi Eze (Malden: Blackwell, 1997): 39.

11. Thomas Jefferson, "The Difference is Fixed in Nature," in Eze, *Race and the Enlightenment*, 102.

12. Georg Wilhelm Friedrich Hegel, "Race, History, and Imperialism," in Eze, *Race and the Enlightenment*, 110.

13. Georg Wilhelm Friedrich Hegel, *Elements of the Philosophy of Right*, ed. Allen W. Wood, trans. H. B. Nisbet (New York: Cambridge University Press, 1991), secs. 341–60.

14. Franz Boas, *The Mind of Primitive Man* (New York: Macmillan, 2011), 255.

15. W. E. B. Du Bois, *The Souls of Black Folk* (New York: Bantam, 1903), 9.

16. Gregory Michael Dorr and Angela Logan, "'Quality, Not Mere Quantity Counts': Black Eugenics and the NAACP Baby Contests," in *A Century of Eugenics in America: From the Indiana Experiment to the Human Genome Era*, ed. Paul Lombardo (Bloomington, IN: Indiana University Press, 2011): 68–92.

17. Michael Omi and Howard Winant, *Racial Formation in the United States* (New York: Routledge, 2015), 54

18. Ibid., 55.

Chapter 1: Post-Racial Theories of Racial Inequality

1. Sheri A. Castro Atwater, "Waking Up to Difference: Teachers, Color Blindness, and the Effects on Students of Color," *Journal of Instructional Psychology* 35, no. 3 (2006): 246–53.

2. Eduardo Bonilla-Silva, *Racism without Racists: Color-Blind Racism and the Persistence of Racial Inequality in the United States* (Lanham, MD: Rowman & Littlefield, 2010), 28.

3. Lawrence Bobo, James R. Kluegel, and Ryan A. Smith, "Laissez-Faire Racism: The Crystallization of a Kinder, Gentler, Anti-Black Ideology," in *Racial Attitudes in the 1990s: Continuity and Change*, ed. Steven A. Tuch and Jack K. Martin (Westport, CT: Praeger, 1997), 15–42.

4. Eric Tranby and Douglas Hartmann, "Critical Whiteness Theories and the Evangelical 'Race Problem': Extending Emerson and Smith's *Divided by Faith*," *Journal for the Scientific Study of Religion* 47, no. 3 (2008): 341–59.

5. Michèle Alexandre, "Black Like Me: One Drop, No Difference?," *Ebony* 66, no. 7 (2011): 91.

6. Alexandre, "Black Like Me," 91.
7. Touré, *Who's Afraid of Post-Blackness?: What It Means to be Black Now* (New York: Simon and Schuster, 2011), 4–7.
8. Stephanie Li, "Black Literary Writers and Post-Blackness," in *The Trouble with Post-Blackness*, ed. Houston A. Baker and K. Merinda Simmons (New York: Columbia University Press, 2015), 44–59.
9. See Manning Marable, "Racializing Obama: The Enigma of Post-Black Politics and Leadership," *Souls* 11, no. 1 (2009): 1–15.
10. K. Merinda Simmons, "Introduction: The Dubious Stage of Post-Blackness—Performing Otherness, Conserving Dominance," in Baker and Simmons, *The Trouble with Post-Blackness*, 1–20.
11. Stephen C. Wright, Donald M. Taylor, and Fathali M. Moghaddam, "Responding to Membership in a Disadvantaged Group: From Acceptance to Collective Protest," *Journal of Personality and Social Psychology* 58, no. 6 (1990): 994–1003.
12. Martijn van Zomeren, Tom Postmes, and Russell Spears, "Toward an Integrative Social Identity Model of Collective Action: A Quantitative Research Synthesis of Three Socio-Psychological Perspectives," *Psychological Bulletin* 134, no. 4 (2008): 504–35.
13. Michael C. Dawson, *Behind the Mule: Race and Class in African-American Politics* (Princeton: Princeton University Press, 1994), 63; Patricia Gurin, Shirley Hatchett, and James S. Jackson, *Hope and Independence: Blacks' Response to Electoral and Party Politics* (New York: R. Sage Foundation, 1989), 17–30; Katherine Tate, *From Protest to Politics: The New Black Voters in American Elections* (New York: Russell Sage, 1993), 20–49.
14. For our purposes, political cohesion is defined as the general tendency among Blacks to agree on certain political issues, particularly policy positions, attitudes, and partisanship.
15. Donald T. Campbell, "Common Fate, Similarity, and Other Indices of the Status of Aggregates of Persons as Social Entities," *Behavioral Science* 3 (1958): 14–25.
16. Dawson, *Behind the Mule*, 76.
17. Kurt Lewin as cited in Gurin et al., *Hope and Independence*, 121–22.
18. Tate, *From Protest to Politics*, 42.
19. Dawson, *Behind the Mule*, 89. The 1984 NBES survey consists of a randomly selected sample of pre- and post-election telephone interviews (1,150 interviews and 872 re-interviews, respectively) for the 1984 election. There was a 58 percent response rate for the total number of attempted interviews. The 1988 NBES consists of 473 pre- and post-election re-interviews of 1984 respondents for the 1988 election. Dawson uses the NBES data set and Gallup opinion poll data in four sets of analyses to construct models of (1) Black racial and economic group

interests; (2) Black partisanship and engagement in the U.S. party system; (3) racial group interests, Black community presidential approval, and macroeconomic policy; (4) and group interests, class divisions, and Black policy preferences.

20. Dawson, *Behind the Mule*, 77, 79.

21. Ibid., 108.

22. Although there were no Black presidents governing during the data periods analyzed by Dawson, the high approval ratings among Blacks, despite stagnated and reversing relative Black unemployment statistics, are inconsistent with the economic realities and predictive powers of the linked-fate model. As of December 2014, according to Gallup, Blacks gave President Obama an 84 percent job approval rating (forty points higher than the overall average), although it had fallen since 2010.

23. Dawson, *Behind the Mule*, 61.

24. Ibid., 186.

25. Christina M. Greer, *Black Ethnics: Race, Immigration, and the Pursuit of the American Dream* (New York: Oxford University Press, 2013), 26.

26. Paradoxically, it seems also that the pronouncement of ethnic Blacks to "elevated minority status" is more of a consolation prize rather than it is an attainment of the American Dream, much the same way that the election of Barack Obama to the American presidency can be viewed as a consolation prize for Black Americans rather than elimination of racism.

27. Greer, *Black Ethnics*, 27.

28. Martin Luther King Jr., "Civil Right Number 1," *New York Times*, March 14, 1965.

29. Frances Fox Piven and Richard A. Cloward, *Why Americans Don't Vote* (New York: Pantheon Press, 1988), xii–xiii.

30. In 2013, the U.S. Supreme Court invalidated section 4 of the Voting Rights Act of 1965, which requires that nine states—Alabama, Alaska, Arizona, Georgia, Louisiana, Mississippi, South Carolina, Texas, and Virginia—and several counties in other states, seek federal approval to change their election laws. It remains to be seen whether this will rekindle Black protest politics.

31. Orlando Patterson, *The Ordeal of Integration: Progress and Resentment in America's "Racial" Crisis* (New York: Basic Civitas, 1997), 99–103; William Julius Wilson, *The Truly Disadvantaged: The Inner City, the Underclass, and Public Policy* (Chicago: University of Chicago Press, 1987), 126–29; William Julius Wilson, *The Declining Significance of Race: Blacks and Changing American Institutions* (Chicago: University of Chicago Press, 1978), 1–2; Eugene Robinson, *Disintegration: The Splintering of Black America* (New York: Doubleday, 2010), 5.

32. Katherine Tate, "Black Political Participation in the 1984 and 1988 Presidential Elections," *American Political Science Review* 85, no. 4 (1991): 1159–76

33. W. E. B. Du Bois, *The Souls of Black Folk* (New York: Bantam, 1903), 3.

34. Enrique Aleman and Sonia M. Aleman, "Do Latin@ Interests Always Have to 'Converge' with White Interests? (Re)claiming Racial Realism and Interest-Convergence in Critical Race Theory Praxis," *Race, Ethnicity and Education* 13, no. 1 (2010): 1–21.

35. Ibid., 2.

36. Louis Graham, Shelly Brown-Jeffy, Robert Aronson, and Charles Stephens, "Critical Race Theory as Theoretical Framework and Analysis Tool for Population Health Research," *Critical Public Health* 21, no. 1 (2011): 81–93.

37. Richard Delgado and Jean Stefancic, *Critical Race Theory: An Introduction* (New York: New York University Press, 2001), 9.

38. Kimberlé Williams Crenshaw, Neil Gotanda, Garry Peller, and Kendall Thomas, eds., "Introduction," in *Critical Race Theory: The Key Writings that Formed the Movement* (New York: New Press, 1995), xiii–xxxii.

39. Bonilla-Silva, *Racism without Racists*, 26.

40. Ibid., 28.

41. Oscar Lewis, "The Culture of Poverty," in *Poor Americans: How the White Poor Live*, ed. Marc Pilisuk and Phyllis Pilisuk (New York: Transaction Books, 1971), 20–26.

42. Bonilla-Silva, *Racism without Racists*, 28.

43. Ibid., 152.

44. Ibid., 30.

Chapter 2: Critical Discourse Analysis and Narratives of Race

1. Teun A. van Dijk, "Critical Discourse Analysis," in *The Handbook of Discourse Analysis*, ed. Deborah Schiffrin, Deborah Tannen, and Heidi E. Hamilton (Malden, MA: Blackwell Publishers Ltd., 2008), 349–71.

2. Ibid., 349.

3. Ibid., 352.

4. Ibid., 355.

5. Ibid., 357–58.

6. Teun A. van Dijk, "Discourse, Power and Access," in *Texts and Practices: Readings in Critical Discourse Analysis*, ed. Carmen Rosa Caldas-Coulthard and Malcolm Coulthard (London: Routledge and Kegan Paul, 1996), 84–104.

7. Ibid., 88–89.

8. Shelby County v. Holder, 570 U.S. ___ (2013).

9. Ibid.
10. Alessandro Duranti and Charles Goodwin, eds., *Rethinking Context: Language as an Interactive Phenomenon* (Cambridge: Cambridge University Press, 1992), 2–3.
11. Ruth Wodak, "'And Where is the Lebanon?' A Socio-psycholinguistic Investigation of Comprehension and Intelligibility of News," *Text 7*, no. 4 (1987): 377–410.
12. Ibid., 380.
13. van Dijk, "Critical Discourse Analysis," 357.
14. Asafa Jalata "Revisiting the Black Struggle: Lessons for the 21st Century," *Journal of Black Studies* 33, no. 1 (2002): 86–116.
15. Stokely Carmichael changed his name to Kwame Ture after moving to West Africa in 1969. I have chosen to refer to him as Stokely Carmichael because early in his activism he was known by that name.
16. Columbus Salley, *A Ranking of the Most Influential African-Americans, Past and Present* (New York: Citadel Press, 1999), 82
17. John H. Bracey, August Meier, and Elliott Rudwick, *Black Nationalism in America* (New York: Bobbs-Merrill, 1970), 299.
18. August Meier and Elliott Rudwick, "Introduction," in *Black Protest Thought in the Twentieth Century*, ed. August Meier, Elliott Rudwick, and Francis L. Broderick (New York: Macmillan, 1985), xix.
19. Bernard Makhosezwe Magubane, *The Ties that Bind: African American Consciousness of Africa* (New Jersey: Africa World Press, 1989), 127.
20. Nathan Irvin Huggins, *Harlem Renaissance* (New York: Oxford University Press, 1971), 79–83.
21. Martin Luther King Jr., *Why We Can't Wait* (New York: Harper & Row, 1964), 33.
22. Manning Marable, *Race, Reform, and Rebellion: The Second Reconstruction in Black America, 1945–2006* (Jackson: University Press of Mississippi, 1991), 80.
23. Ibid., 84–90.
24. Gene Marine, *The Black Panthers* (New York: New American Library, 1986), 35–36.
25. Anthony D. Smith, *National Identity* (Las Vegas: University of Nevada Press, 1991), 99.
26. Anthony Oberschall, *Social Conflict and Social Movements* (Englewood Cliffs, NJ: Prentice Hall, 1973), 223–226.
27. Doug McAdam, John D. McCarthy, and Mayer N. Zald, "Social Movements," in *Handbook of Sociology*, ed. Neil. J. Smelser (Newbury Park, CA: Sage, 1998), 695–737.
28. Martin Luther King Jr., *Strength to Love* (New York: Pocket Books, 1964), 80.

29. James Farmer, *Lay Bare the Heart: An Autobiography of the Civil Rights Movement* (New York: Arbor House, 1985), 187–188.

30. Ibid., 215.

31. King, *Strength to Love*, 14.

32. Ira G. Zepp, *The Social Vision of Martin Luther King, Jr.* (New York: Carlson, 1989), 54.

33. Marable, *Race, Reform, and Rebellion*, 105.

34. Robert Allen, *Reluctant Reformers: Racism and Social Reform Movements in the United States* (Washington, DC: Howard University Press, 1983), 322.

Chapter 3: Ebullience and Action in Black Discourse

1. Martin Luther King Jr., "A Realistic Look at the Question of Progress in the Area of Race Relations" (speech, St. Louis, MO, April 10, 1957), https://kinginstitute.stanford.edu/king-papers/documents/realistic-look -question-progress-area-race-relations-address-delivered-st.

2. Ibid.

3. Ibid.

4. Ibid.

5. Ibid.

6. Ibid.

7. Martin Luther King Jr., "Give Us the Ballot" (speech, Washington, DC, May 17, 1957), http://kingencyclopedia.stanford.edu/encyclopedia /document sentry/doc_give_us_the_ballot_address_at_the_prayer_pil grimage_for_freedom/.

8. Ibid.

9. Ibid.

10. Martin Luther King Jr., "The Other America" (speech, Grosse Pointe, MI, March 14, 1968), http://www.gphistorical.org/mlk/mlkspeech/.

11. Ibid.

12. Ibid., emphasis added.

13. Ibid.

14. Ibid.

15. Ibid.

16. Ibid.

17. Ibid.

18. Ibid.

19. Ibid.

20. Ibid.

21. Martin Luther King Jr., "I've Been to the Mountaintop" (speech, Memphis, TN, April 3, 1968), http://www.americanrhetoric.com/speeches /mlkivebeentothemountaintop.htm.

22. Ibid.
23. Ibid.
24. Ibid.
25. Ibid.
26. King, "A Realistic Look."
27. Ibid.
28. King, "Give Us the Ballot."
29. Ibid.
30. King, "I've Been to the Mountaintop."
31. Malcolm X, "The Ballot or the Bullet" (speech, Cleveland, OH, April 3, 1964, before the passage of the Civil Rights Act of 1964), http://www .edchange.org/multicultural/speeches/malcolm_x_ballot.html.
32. Ibid.
33. The reference here is to Lyndon B. Johnson's administration.
34. Malcolm X, "The Ballot or the Bullet."
35. Malcolm X, "After the Bombing" (speech, Detroit, MI, February 14, 1965), http://www.malcolm-x.org/speeches/spc_021465.htm.
36. Ibid.
37. Ibid.
38. Ibid.
39. Ibid.
40. Stokely Carmichael, "Black Power" (speech, Berkeley, CA, October 29, 1966), http://voicesofdemocracy.umd.edu/carmichael-black-power-speech -text/.
41. Ibid.
42. Ibid.
43. Ibid.
44. Ibid.
45. Ibid.
46. John McWhorter, *Losing the Race: Self-Sabotage in Black America* (New York: Harper Perennial, 2001), xiv.
47. Ibid., 42.
48. Ibid., x.
49. Ibid., 21.
50. Ibid., xi, 50.
51. Ibid., 51
52. Ibid., 51, 53.
53. Ibid., 65.
54. Ibid., 83.
55. Ibid., xii.
56. Ibid., 83.
57. Ibid., 88.

58. Ibid., 162.
59. John H. McWhorter, *Winning the Race: Beyond the Crisis in Black America* (New York: Gotham Books, 2005).
60. Ibid., 6.
61. Ibid., 172.
62. Ibid., 164–65.
63. Eric Hoffer, *The True Believer: Thoughts on the Nature of Mass Movements* (New York: Harper and Row, 1951), 79–106.
64. McWhorter, *Winning the Race*, 7.
65. Ibid., 162.
66. Ibid., 120.
67. Ibid., 263, 352–58, 363–65.
68. Ron Eyerman, *Cultural Trauma: Slavery and the Formation of African American Identity* (Cambridge: Cambridge University Press, 2001), 1–2.
69. William Mangino, "Race to College: The Reverse Gap." *Race and Social Problems* 2 (December 2010): 164–78.
70. John Bound and Richard B. Freeman, "What Went Wrong? The Erosion of Relative Earnings and Employment among Young Black Men in the 1980s," *Quarterly Journal of Economics* 107, no. 1 (1992): 201–32.
71. William Darity Jr. and Darrick Hamilton, "Bold Policies for Economic Justice," *Review of Black Political Economy* 39, no. 1 (2012): 79–85.
72. Ibid., 80.
73. Karolyn Tyson, William Darity Jr., and Domini R. Castellino, "It's Not 'a Black Thing': Understanding the Burden of Acting White and Other Dilemmas of High Achievement," *American Sociological Review* 70, no. 4 (2005), 582–605.
74. Tyson et al., "It's Not 'a Black Thing,'" 589.
75. Andra Gillespie, *Whose Black Politics?: Cases in Post-Racial Black Leadership* (New York: Routledge, 2010), 20.
76. Ibid., 9.
77. Ibid.,14.
78. Ibid., 56.
79. Ibid., 2.
80. Ibid., 312.
81. Terry H. Anderson, *The Pursuit of Fairness: A History of Affirmative Action* (New York: Oxford University Press, 2004), 167.
82. Gillespie, *Whose Black Politics?*, 22.
83. Ibid., 22–25.
84. Ibid., 31.
85. Ibid., 22.
86. Ibid., 36.
87. Ibid., 15.

88. Ibid., 11.
89. Ibid., 310.
90. Ibid., 311.
91. Barack Obama, "Morehouse College Commencement Speech" (Atlanta, GA, May 19, 2013), http://www.ajc.com/news/local/prepared-text-for-president-obama-speech-morehouse/82cVEdUTCaJA6SixsyKWIN/.
92. Ibid.
93. Ibid.
94. Ibid.
95. Ibid.
96. Ibid.
97. Fredrick Harris, *The Price of the Ticket: Barack Obama and Rise and Decline of Black* (New York: Oxford University Press, 2012), 101.
98. Obama, "Morehouse College Commencement Speech."
99. Ibid.
100. Ibid.
101. Ibid.
102. King's criticism of the hypocritical policy to give land grants and subsidies to White farmers while denying government support to Blacks could even be viewed as "making excuses" for individuals' failure to achieve economic success.
103. Obama, "Morehouse College Commencement Speech."
104. Barack Obama, "Barnard College Commencement Speech" (New York, May 14, 2012), https://barnard.edu/headlines/transcript-speech-president-barack-obama.
105. Ibid.
106. Ibid.
107. Ibid.
108. Barack Obama, "Speech to the 99th Annual Convention of the NAACP" (Cincinnati, OH, July 14, 2008), http://www.presidency.ucsb.edu/ws/index.php?pid=77650.
109. Ibid.
110. Ibid.
111. Ibid.
112. Ibid.
113. Ibid.
114. Ibid.
115. Ibid.
116. Harris, *The Price of the Ticket,* 153.
117. Obama, "Morehouse College Commencement Speech."
118. As of May 2013, the seasonally adjusted unemployment rate for Black men twenty years and older was 13.5 percent as compared to 6.3

percent for White men in the same age range. The reality is, for Blacks in general and Black men particularly, job-market opportunities have been consistently bleak, and there has been a persistent two-to-one racial unemployment gap.

119. Obama, "Morehouse College Commencement Speech."
120. Obama, "Barnard College Commencement Speech."
121. Ibid.
122. Ibid.
123. Ibid.
124. Obama, "Speech to the 99th Annual Convention of the NAACP."
125. Eddie S. Glaude Jr., "The Problem of African American Public(s): Dewey and African American Politics in the 21st Century," *Contemporary Pragmatism* 7 (2010): 9–29.
126. Teun A. van Dijk, *Critical Discourse Analysis: The Handbook of Discourse Analysis* (Malden, MA: Blackwell, 2008), 349–71.
127. Michael Dawson, *Behind the Mule: Race and Class in African-American Politics* (Princeton: ton University Press, 1994), 204, 205; Katherine Tate, "Black political participation in the 1984 and 1988 presidential elections," *American Political Science Review* 85, no. 4 (1991): 1159–76.
128. Christina M. Greer, *Black Ethnics: Race, Immigration, and the Pursuit of the American Dream* (New York: Oxford University Press, 2013), 55–60.
129. Greer, *Black Ethnics*, 112.

Chapter 4: Social Knowledge and Black "Progress"

1. Pew Research Center, *Blacks Upbeat about Black Progress, Prospects* (Washington, DC: Pew Research Center, 2010), http://www.pewsocial trends.org/2010/01/12/blacks-upbeatabout-black-progress-prospects/, par. 12.
2. Ibid., par. 14.
3. Rebecca Tippett, Avis Jones-DeWeever, Maya Rockeymoore, Darrick Hamilton, and William Darity Jr., "Beyond Broke: Why Closing the Racial Wealth Gap is a Priority for National Economic Security," *Center for Global Policy Solutions*, 2014, http://globalpolicysolutions.org /wp-content/uploads/2014/04/BeyondBroke_Exec_Summary.pdf, 4.
4. Fredrick C. Harris, *Something Within: Religion in African-American Political Activism* (New York: Oxford University Press, 1999), 6–7.
5. Fredrick C. Harris, "Something Within: Religion as a Mobilizer of African-American Political Activism," *Journal of Politics* 56, no. 1 (1994): 42–68.
6. Harris, *Something Within*, 42.
7. Ibid., 43–44.

8. Kareem U. Crayton, "The Art of Racial Dissent: African American Political Discourse in the Age of Obama," *Chicago-Kent Law Review* 89 no. 2 (2014): 695.

9. W. E. B. Du Bois, *The Souls of Black Folk* (New York: Bantam, 1903), 13.

10. Ibid., 13.

11. Melissa Victoria Harris-Lacewell, *Barbershops, Bibles, and BET: Everyday Talk and Black Political Thought* (Princeton: Princeton University Press, 2004), xxii.

12. Mia Smith Bynum, Candace Best, Sandra L. Barnes, and E. Thomoseo Burton, "Private Regard, Identity Protection and Perceived Racism among African American Males," *Journal of African American Studies* 12, no. 2 (2008): 142–55.

13. Ibid., 151.

14. Donald P. Haider-Markel, William Delehanty, and Matthew Beverlin, "Media Framing and Racial Attitudes in the Aftermath of Katrina," *Policy Studies Journal* 35, no. 4 (2007): 587–605.

15. Ibid., 590.

16. Alexander M. Czopp and Margo J. Monteith, "Thinking Well of African Americans: Measuring Complimentary Stereotypes and Negative Prejudice," *Basic and Applied Social Psychology* 28, no. 3 (2006): 233–50.

17. Barack Obama, "Morehouse College Commencement Speech" (Atlanta, GA, May 19, 2013), http://www.ajc.com/news/local/prepared-text-for-president-obama-speech-morehouse/82cVEdUTCaJA6SixsyK WIN/.

18. Stephen Ellingson, "Understanding the Dialectic of Discourse and Collective Action: Public Debate and Rioting in Antebellum Cincinnati," *American Journal of Sociology* 101, no. 1 (1995): 100–44.

19. Ibid., 137.

20. Michael Owens, *God and Government in the Ghetto: The Politics of Church-State Collaboration in Black America* (Chicago: University of Chicago Press, 2008), 3–4.

21. As articulated in Kareem U. Crayton, "The Art of Racial Dissent: African American Political Discourse in the Age of Obama," *Chicago-Kent Law Review* 89, no. 2 (2014): 695.

22. Amandia Speakes-Lewis, Leroy L. Gill, and Crystal George Moses, "The Move Toward American Modernity: Empowerment and Individualism in the Black Mega Church," *Journal of African American Studies* 15, no. 2 (2011): 245.

23. Riva Renee Brown, "Trayvon Martin and Election 2012 Social Media Messaging: An Analysis of Framing, Rhetoric, and Media Types in Online Messages by Civil Rights Organizations," *Dissertations* (2013), http://aquila.usm.edu/dissertations/164.

24. Charles P. Henry, "Herman Cain and the Rise of the Black Right," *Journal of Black Studies* 44, no. 6 (2013): 551–71.

25. Carol Graham, "The Surprising Optimism of Black Americans," *Brookings Social Mobility Memos* (September 25, 2015), http://www.brookings.edu/blogs/social-mobility-memos/posts/2015/09/25-surprising-optimism-black-americans-graham, par. 9.

Chapter 5: Black America at the End of the Obama Era

1. john a. powell, "Post-Racialism or Targeted Universalism," *Denver University Law Review* 86 (2008): 785–806.

2. The U.S. Supreme Court 2013 ruling on the Voting Rights Act of 1965 is an example that illustrates my point. The ruling invalidated section 4 of the Voting Rights Act, thus making it effectively impossible to enforce section 5, which deals with preclearance. Thus the policy is unable to provide its intended beneficiaries with the intended benefits.

3. Rachael Faithful, "#BlackLivesMatter Kitchen Talk," *National Lawyers Guild Review* 71, no. 4 (2014): 246–56.

4. Jamiles Lartey, "Obama on Black Lives Matter: They Are 'Much Better Organizers Than I Was,'" *The Guardian*, February 18, 2016, http://www.theguardian.com/us-news/2016/feb/18/black-lives-matter-meet-president-obama-white-house-justice-system, par. 11.

5. Jennifer Senior, "The Paradox of the First Black President," *New York Magazine*, October 7, 2015, http://nymag.com/daily/intelligencer/2015/10/paradox-of-the-first-black-president.html, par. 28.

6. Ibid., par 8.

7. Frank Vyan Welton, "Daily Beast Claims 'Black Lives Matter Is Living in the Past,'" *Daily Kos,* September 30, 2015, http://www.dailykos.com/story/2015/9/30/1426281/-Daily-Beast-claims-BlackLivesMatter-is-Living-in-the-Past, par. 2.

8. Quoted in Senior, "Paradox of the First Black President," par. 9.

9. Russell Rickford, "Black Lives Matter: Toward a Modern Practice of Mass Struggle," *New Labor Forum* 25, no. 1 (2016): 34–42.

10. Alan Aja, Daniel Bustillo, William Darity Jr., and Darrick Hamilton, "Jobs Instead of Austerity: A Bold Policy Proposal for Economic Justice," *Social Research: an International Quarterly* 80, no. 3 (2013): 781–94.

11. William Darity Jr. and Darrick Hamilton, "Bold Policies for Economic Justice," *Review of Black Political Economy* 39, no. 1 (2012): 79–85; Alan Aja, Daniel Bustillo, William Darity Jr., and Darrick Hamilton, "From a Tangle of Pathology to a Race Fair America," *Dissent Magazine* (Summer 2014), http://www.dissentmagazine.org/article/from-a-tangle-of-pathology-to-a-race-fair-america, par. 23.

12. Alberto Alesina, Edward Glaeser, and Bruce Sacerdote, "Why Doesn't the United States Have a European-Style Welfare State?" *Brookings Papers on Economic Activity* 2 (2001): 187–277.

13. Ibid., 189.

14. Ibid., 187.

15. Theda Skocpol, "Targeting within Universalism: Politically Viable Policies to Combat Poverty in the United States," in *The Urban Underclass*, ed. Christopher Jencks and Paul E. Peterson (Washington, DC: Brookings Institution, 1991), 411–36.

16. powell, "Post-Racialism or Targeted Universalism," 805–6.

17. Darity and Hamilton, "Bold Policies for Economic Justice," 79–85.

18. Ibid., 84.

19. Aja et al., "Jobs Instead of Austerity," 790.

20. Robin J. Hayes, "'A Free Black Mind is a Concealed Weapon' Institutions and Social Movements in the African Diaspora," *Souls* 9, no. 3 (2007): 223–34.

21. William Mangino, "Race to College: The Reverse Gap," *Race and Social Problems* 2 (2010), 164–78; Patrick L. Mason, "Race, Culture, and Skill: Interracial Wage Differences among African Americans, Latinos, and Whites," *Review of Black Political Economy* 25, no. 3 (1997): 5–39.

22. Karolyn Tyson, William Darity Jr., and Domini R. Castellino, "It's Not 'a Black Thing': Understanding the Burden of Acting White and Other Dilemmas of High Achievement," *American Sociological Review* 70, no. 4 (2005), 582–605.

23. Aja et al. "Jobs Instead of Austerity," 785–86.

24. Barack Obama, "Farewell Address," (Chicago, IL, January 20, 2017), https://obamawhitehouse.archives.gov/farewell, par. 9.

Epilogue: The Role of Elite Discourse in the Trump Era and Beyond

1. Michael C. Dawson, *Behind the Mule: Race and Class in African-American Politics* (Princeton: Princeton University Press, 1994).

2. Jeremy Diamond, "Trump: Black Communities in Worst Shape 'Ever, Ever, Ever,'" *CNN Politics*, September 20, 2016, http://www.cnn.com/2016/09/20/politics/donald-trump-african-americans-election-2016/index.html.

3. Kristen McQueary, "The Truth of Donald Trump's Message: Black Lives Do Matter," *Chicago Tribune*, July 22, 2016, http://www.chicagotribune.com/news/opinion/commentary/ct-cleveland-trump-rnc-black-lives-matte-police-mcqueary-perspec-0724-jm-20160722-story.html.

4. Leon Neyfakh, "In One of His First Acts as President, Donald Trump Put Black Lives Matter on Notice," *Slate*, January 20, 2017, http:

//www.slate.com/blogs/the_slatest/2017/01/20/donald_trump_puts
_black_lives_matter_on_notice.html.

5. Cleve R. Wootson Jr., "Trump Implied Frederick Douglass Was Alive.
The Abolitionist's Family Offered a 'History Lesson,'" *Washington Post,*
February 2, 2017, https://www.washingtonpost.com/news/post-nation
/wp/2017/02/02/trump-implied-frederick-douglass-was-alive-the-abo
litionists-family-offered-a-history-lesson/?utm_term=.933ed f8e4foa.

6. Jacey Fortin, "Trump's Black History Talk: From Douglass to Media Bias
and Crime," *New York Times,* February 1, 2017, https://www.nytimes
.com/2017 /02/01/us/politics/trump-black-history-douglass.html.

7. Emanuella Grinberg, "DeVos under Fire for Calling HBCUs 'Pioneers'
of School Choice," *CNN,* February 28, 2017, http://www.cnn.com/2017/02
/28/politics/betsy-devos-hbcu-school-choice/index.html.

8. Liam Stack, "Ben Carson Refers to Slaves as 'Immigrants' in First
Remarks to HUD Staff," *New York Times,* March 6, 2017, https://www
.nytimes.com/2017/03/06/us/politics/ben-carson-refers-to-slaves-as-im
migrants-in-first-remarks-to-hud-staff.html, para. 1.

9. "Alveda King gives Trump an 'A' on Race Relations in His First 100
Days," *Fox News,* April 29, 2017, http://insider.foxnews.com/2017/04/29
/alveda-king-gives-trump-race-relations-his-first-100-days.

10. Chandelis R. Duster, "Congressional Black Caucus to Highlight
Trump Admin's Racial Problems with #StayWoke Campaign," *NBC
News,* April 27, 2017, http://www.nbcnews.com/storyline/president
-trumps-first-100-days/congressional-black-caucus-highlight-trump
-admin-s-racial-problems-staywoke-n752266.

11. Jamiles Lartey, "Congressional Black Caucus Refuses to Meet with
Donald Trump," *The Guardian,* June 21, 2017, https://www.theguardian
.com/us-news/2017/jun/21/donald-trump-congressional-black-caucus
-no-meeting.

12. Duster, "Congressional Black Caucus to Highlight Trump Admin's
Racial Problems."

13. Philip Bump, "The Unusual Split in Perceptions of Race Relations
between Donald Trump and Barack Obama," *Washington Post,* July 12,
2016, https://www.washingtonpost.com/news/the-fix/wp/2016/07/12/the
-unusual-split-in-perceptions-of-race-relations-between-donald\trump
-and-barack-obama/.

14. Pew Research Center, "How Blacks and Whites View the State of Race
in America," *Pew Research Center,* June 24, 2016, http://www.pewsocial
trends.org/interactives/state-of-race-in-america/.

INDEX

DR. LESSIE BRANCH is a racial policy scholar and Fulbright Specialist in race, ethnicity, and religion and senior research fellow at the DuBois Bunche Center for Public Policy at Medgar Evers College. She is also on faculty at Monroe College in the social sciences department.

Branch has a PhD in philosophy from the Milano School of International Affairs, Management, and Urban Policy, an MA in political science from the New School for Social Research and a BA in political science from Fordham University.

Her research examines the gulf between Black optimism about group progress and the actual data on continuing disparities and potentially speaks to wider questions of social knowledge, social beliefs and relative group position—even to questions of "consciousness" and ontology.

Branch lives with her husband, David L. Branch I, in Westchester County, New York. Their son, David L. Branch II, is a product design major at Parsons School of Design.